WELL PLAYED

Building Mathematical Thinking Through Number Games and Puzzles

GRADES 3–5

Linda Dacey, Karen Gartland, and Jayne Bamford Lynch

Foreword by Kassia Omohundro Wedekind

Stenhouse
PUBLISHERS

www.stenhouse.com

Portland, Maine

Stenhouse Publishers
www.stenhouse.com

Library of Congress Cataloging-in-Publication Data

Dacey, Linda Schulman, 1949–

Well played: building mathematical thinking through number games and puzzles, grades 3–5 / Linda Dacey, Karen Gartland, and Jayne Bamford Lynch.

pages cm

Includes bibliographical references.

ISBN 978-1-62531-032-3 (pbk.: alk. paper)
– ISBN 978-1-62531-060-6 (ebook)
1. Mathematics–Study and teaching (Elementary)
2. Games in mathematics education.
3. Mathematical recreations. I. Gartland, Karen.
II. Lynch, Jayne Bamford. III. Title.

QA135.6.D3325 2015

372.7'049–dc23

2014048599

Cover design by Alessandra S. Turati

Interior design and typesetting by Victory Productions, Inc.

Manufactured in the United States of America

PRINTED ON 30% PCW
RECYCLED PAPER

21 20 19 18 17   9 8 7 6 5 4 3 2

CONTENTS

Foreword by Kassia Omohundro Wedekind   vi

Acknowledgments   viii

Chapter 1: Introduction   1

     Why This Book?   2

     Is It a Game or a Puzzle or an Activity?   3

     How Is This Book Organized?   3

Chapter 2: Supporting Learning Through Games and Puzzles   5

     Using Games and Puzzles in the Classroom   6

     Setting Expectations and Sharing Responsibilities with Students   7

     Assessing Learning and Setting Goals   12

     Fostering Productive Discussions   16

     Meeting Individual Differences   17

     Organizing Students for Success   18

     Organizing Materials for Success   21

     Working with Families   22

     Conclusion   23

Chapter 3: Base Ten Numeration   25

     Which Number Is Closest?   26

     The Number Is/What Number Is?   30

     Mystery Number   33

     Get to One or One-Tenth   37

     Can You Make This Number?   41

     Online Games and Apps   44

Chapter 4: Addition and Subtraction   47

     What's Your Problem?   48

     Tic-Tic-Tac-Toe   52

     Logical Numbers   56

     Subtracto Draw   59

     Double Decimal Dilemma   63

     Online Games and Apps   67

Chapter 5: Multiplication and Division **69**

Table Topper 70
Five of a Kind 74
Equal Values 77
Think Remainder 81
Matchups 84
Online Games and Apps 88

Chapter 6: Mixed Operations **91**

Roll Six 92
Write It Right 97
Decade Roll 101
Calculator Target 105
Contig 108
Online Games and Apps 112

Chapter 7: Fractions **115**

Unit Fractions and Wholes 116
Name That Number 121
Order Up 125
Fraction Action 128
Fraction Jigsaw 132
Online Games and Apps 135

Appendix **A-1**
Puzzle Answer Key **219**
References **221**

Games and Puzzles Listed in Alphabetical Order

	Description	Appendix
Calculator Target	105	A-59
Can You Make This Number?	41	A-16
Contig	108	A-62
Decade Roll	101	A-57
Double Decimal Dilemma	63	A-29
Equal Values	77	A-40
Five of a Kind	74	A-33
Fraction Action	128	A-76
Fraction Jigsaw	132	A-79
Get to One or One-Tenth	37	A-14
Logical Numbers	56	A-23
Matchups	84	A-48
Mystery Number	33	A-10
Name That Number	121	A-68
The Number Is/What Number Is?	30	A-7
Order Up	125	A-72
Roll Six	92	A-51
Subtracto Draw	59	A-26
Table Topper	70	A-31
Think Remainder	81	A-45
Tic-Tic-Tac-Toe	52	A-20
Unit Fractions and Wholes	116	A-65
What's Your Problem?	48	A-18
Which Number Is Closest?	26	A-4
Write It Right	97	A-53

FOREWORD

When I first opened this book, I remember thinking, "How will this book about math games and puzzles be different from the countless other resources on the topic?" Only a few pages in, I realized that *Well Played* is very different. This is a book about math games and puzzles, but it is also a book about building communities of mathematicians who work together to problem solve, talk about math, and figure things out. This is a book full of thoughtful and well-chosen games and puzzles, but it is also a book that offers a lens into how we might include this kind of play in our own classrooms in ways that are deeply meaningful and engaging for our students. It is a book truly rooted in the realities and possibilities of the classroom, which is what makes it such a valuable resource for teachers.

Well Played includes games and puzzles that check all the boxes for inclusion in the classroom—simple to learn but mathematically meaningful, variations that allow for differentiation within the classroom, and nuanced enough to allow students to expand upon and deepen thinking through multiple experiences with the game over time.

There are several parts of each game or puzzle's description to which readers will want to pay special attention. Each "How It Looks in the Classroom" section offers a glimpse into a classroom in which the game or puzzle is being introduced or played. Going beyond how to play the game, these sections offer teachers ideas for launching the game or puzzle in ways that encourage curiosity, collaboration, math talk, and productive struggle.

Each "What to Look For" section offers several questions for teachers to consider as they work with students. I can imagine keeping these questions on my clipboard as I observe and confer with students as a way of guiding my instructional moves and helping me take useful anecdotal notes on students' strategies and understandings.

Each game or puzzle includes exit card questions to use for student reflection. These questions offer an opportunity for students to synthesize and solidify understandings through writing; they also offer teachers the opportunity to assess students' understanding and use this knowledge to plan next steps for instruction. Carefully chosen student work examples provide a reference point for teachers as they analyze and respond to student thinking.

One of my favorite games in this book is "Get to One or One-Tenth," from Chapter 3, "Base Ten Numeration." Developing an understanding of place value and base ten with whole numbers is an important focus of the primary grades. However, it is often wrongly assumed that students automatically transfer this understanding to decimal numbers in the upper grades. Older students need time and space to explore and make connections that allow them to fully understand our base ten number system, and this game helps facilitate this critical understanding. Two versions of this game build upon whole number understanding and familiar tools, allowing students to explore the relationships between ones, tenths, hundredths, and thousandths. Time spent with this game will help lay the important foundational understanding for later work with decimal computation.

Well Played also acknowledges the powerful potential of online math play, offering suggestions for games, puzzles, and apps at the end of each chapter. Though many online games focus on skill-and-drill and fluency practice, the authors have chosen games and puzzles that emphasize problem solving and offer students opportunities to model with mathematics.

While this book will be a prized resource of classroom teachers, as a blend of professional development and practical resources, it will also be valued by coaches as they work with teachers to deepen content understanding and guide instructional practices.

As I read this book I kept thinking, "I can't wait to see what students will do with this game!" and "I know a teacher who will love using this puzzle with her class!" I know my copy of this book with soon be full of sticky notes and dog-eared pages, and a list of people with whom I want to share it. I know teachers will love this book as much as I do—thank you Linda, Karen, and Jayne for writing it!

Kassia Omohundro Wedekind, author of *Math Exchanges: Guiding Young Mathematicians in Small-Group Meetings*

Acknowledgments

We are deeply indebted to the teachers and students who collaborated with us during the development of this project. Each game was explored within a classroom, and teacher and student insights permeate this book. We are particularly grateful to students for serving as our consumer experts. Their feedback helped us fine-tune our thinking and play more with ways to embed key mathematical ideas into our discussions of the games and puzzles.

We are grateful to everyone at Stenhouse, but most particularly Toby Gordon, who showed such early faith in us. Her words "Write about what matters most to you" gave us the freedom to explore, reflect, play, and puzzle. And then, of course, she gave us such valuable and timely feedback all along the way. We are also grateful to our outstanding outside reviewer, who probed our thinking with important insights and intriguing questions. Thank you also to Chris Downey, Elizabeth Tripp, and Jay Kilburn for their care and expertise. All of you added greatly to the quality of our work.

We have great respect for Kassia Omohundro Wedekind's work and are honored by her words in the foreword.

CHAPTER 1

Introduction

It is a happy talent to know how to play.
—Ralph Waldo Emerson

Our whole life is solving puzzles.
—Erno Rubik

Did you have a favorite game or puzzle as a child? Why did you like it? Looking back, what do you think you learned from it?

People have engaged in playing games and solving puzzles for thousands of years. Games and puzzles continue to provide important opportunities for children to experience structured play. And, as the proliferation of online game playing and puzzle solving shows, these activities continue to capture our interest.

Games and puzzles based on logical thinking are often linked to mathematics. Out of school, they are considered recreational. In school, they often provide opportunities for students to practice skills. We see their incorporation in math lessons more than in other subject areas. Within mathematics, they tend to focus on computation, with the goal of increasing fluency. Games and puzzles are included in most mathematics curriculum resources, and teachers might offer them as a choice at a center, as an independent activity during math workshop, or as a rotation during instructional time.

Why This Book?

So, with interest in games and puzzles fully established and lots of games available to teachers through online sources and curriculum materials, why did we want to write this book? As a way to begin to answer this question, we'd like to share something we witnessed in a fourth-grade classroom when we asked a teacher to have her students play *Get to One*, a game we adapted from a popular game usually played with whole numbers.

Eight students were individually playing *Get to One* (see page 37), a game requiring players to begin at 0, roll a die, and then make a calculated decision as to whether to count forward that number of tenths or that number of hundredths. Play continues until the player reaches 1.00 on the hundredths board. To support accountability, students must record their rolls, whether they assigned tenths or hundredths to the numbers, and their new positions on the board. The teacher asked these students to each play one or two games and to place a completed game sheet in the folder before rotating to their next assigned location.

We noted that one student, Quinn, was on 0.97 and rolled a 5. He recorded that he would assign it the value of hundredths and counted forward, "Ninety-seven, 98, 99, 100, 101, 102 hundredths." On his recording sheet he wrote that he would end his turn on 0.102, but then he couldn't find that number on the board. He decided that 0.12 looked the closest and moved his chip back to that place. He did not record his subsequent turns until he moved forward to 0.96 and, fortunately, rolled a 4. As a result, Quinn completed only one game, while the others had time to play two, and his misconception remained undetected.

We know it is impossible for teachers to monitor all students all of the time, but observing Quinn caused us to think more about the use of games and puzzles in our classrooms. We began with the question *How could we increase the likelihood that this misunderstanding would be noticed and addressed?* Our conversation then moved quickly to a general discussion about games and puzzles and how we could increase their potential for deepening students' conceptual learning as well as their computational fluency. It wasn't long before we knew that we had discovered our next project.

We began our work by identifying our favorite games and puzzles and asking teachers to do the same. Then we tried to think about how to deepen student learning through their exploration. We asked ourselves key questions, including

> ❭ Why is this game or puzzle worth exploring?
> ❭ How could student-to-student math talk be increased?
> ❭ What might teachers notice as students played the game or solved the puzzle that would inform future instruction?
> ❭ What assessment tasks could reinforce student accountability?
> ❭ What task would provide an opportunity to extend students' thinking?

Is It a Game or a Puzzle or an Activity?

One of the surprises of this work was how murky the distinctions can be among games, puzzles, and tasks. Is a computer game that requires a player to find clues and the correct path to reach a certain goal a game or a series of puzzles? Are we playing a game when we solve a puzzle? Is pinning decimal numbers in order along a clothesline a puzzle, a task, or a game? Koster suggests that "games are puzzles to solve, just like everything else we encounter in life" (2013, 34). Note that both games and puzzles

- involve sequencing and pattern recognition;
- require strategy; and
- offer competition against an opponent, or clock, or your own abilities to reach a solution.

There are, of course, some differences. For example, puzzles can be lost only by giving up. We have identified the games and puzzles in this book as either one or the other, but we found the following criteria important to both:

- It addresses important mathematical ideas.
- It is engaging.
- It offers a range of difficulty levels.
- It requires and stimulates mathematical insight.
- It supports the habits of mind essential for success with mathematics and real-world problem solving.

How Is This Book Organized?

Chapter 2 addresses instructional decisions related to games and puzzles in the classroom. Our goal is to support teacher orchestration of gaming and puzzling as well as assessment of student learning. We pay particular attention to helping students take responsibility for their roles as players and puzzlers. Kohlfeld (2009) also identifies the need to instruct students in how to choose partners, take turns, be patient, and lose. We would add to this list teaching students how to work cooperatively, discuss ideas, persevere, and win graciously. All of these ideas are considered in Chapter 2.

The next five chapters of this book focus on content-specific games and puzzles arranged by content focus: base ten numeration; addition and subtraction; multiplication and division; mixed operations; and fractions. Whole numbers and decimals are included in the first four of these chapters, and the fraction chapter includes both developing conceptual understanding of fractions and computing with them. There are five fully developed games or puzzles within each chapter as well as a section that considers online games and puzzles (including apps). The online section is more general as such resources change so frequently. Within this section, we identify those electronic resources that are free.

The discussion of each game and puzzle is organized to address the goals we identified when we began this project. Along with the expected sections "Math Focus" and "Directions," each discussion includes a section called "How It Looks in the Classroom," which shares a brief classroom story from our field testing. "Tips from the Classroom" provides further ideas for supporting classroom implementation, some of which came from our student field testers. "What to Look For" identifies key ideas and misunderstandings that our experience suggests will be tapped, allowing you to collect data to inform instructional decisions and note student growth over time. The "Variations" section suggests ways to change the game or puzzle to further reach the range of learners in your class. The section "Exit Card Choices" provides some suggested questions you can pose to students after their experience with a game or puzzle. The tasks serve as a way for students to bring closure to the experience while demonstrating their knowledge. Such questions reinforce student accountability for their own learning. Students' responses support your instructional decision-making.

As teachers, we recognize the value in partnering with students about their learning. The more we communicate to students the role that games and puzzles play in supporting their understanding of key mathematical concepts and the use of mathematics in the real world, the better. Recording sheets and exit cards allow students to share their strategies and knowledge and provide teachers with the opportunity to assess learning. At the end of each game or puzzle discussion, the "Extension" section, as you would expect, gives you an idea for extending the learning. As you gain familiarity, you, or your students, may create other examples of such questions and tasks.

No doubt you may be familiar with some of the games and puzzles included in this resource, especially those that are classics; you have your own favorites, too. Nonetheless, we are confident that you will appreciate the opportunity to think about the use of games and puzzles in the classroom and find new ways to make their exploration more effective for engaging students and deepening mathematical understanding.

Supporting Learning Through Games and Puzzles

As students enter their fourth-grade classroom they read the morning message, which tells them to sign up for a math activity choice before they begin their "do now" assignment. Sara and Mariana are looking at the choice board. Sara says, "I think I should sign up for Table Topper. *Want to play it with me?"*

Mariana pauses a moment and then says, "I need to meet my division goal. I am going to choose Five of a Kind. *Let's sit together at morning meeting."*

As simple as this scene may appear to an outside observer, teachers know that it reflects deep values related to students sharing responsibility for their learning. Teachers will also recognize the instilling of routines and setting of expectations that must precede such behavior. Thoughtful orchestration of mathematical games and puzzles goes well beyond offering opportunities to play and solve. We need to think about when and how to introduce games and puzzles and when to make them available for small-group or individual use. We must help students understand the purposes of and expectations for playing and solving and look for ways to share the responsibility of the learning process with them. We want to set and assess learning goals, support math talk, and meet the needs of individual learners while pursuing such activities. We should recognize ways to organize students and materials to support success, and we want to involve families and caregivers in the playing and solving.

Using Games and Puzzles in the Classroom

We believe that the instructional potential of games and puzzles could be further realized in most classrooms. Often we've seen them provided as activities with little follow-up or offered to students as choices after they have mastered the related mathematical content. We've seen that teachers who implement good teaching practices, such as asking significant debriefing questions after a problem-solving experience, often fall short of utilizing such practices with games and puzzles. Further, the games and puzzles used most frequently in classrooms tend to only develop procedural expertise, without attending to conceptual understanding. As a result, many students experience games or puzzles as fun activities or time fillers, but do not consider them as essential to their learning or as an important part of a lesson for which they are accountable.

Many teachers provide a game or puzzle station as a component of a three-rotation lesson structure (small-group meeting with teacher, independent work, and game or puzzle). Some educators recommend an instructional cycle similar to that shown in Figure 2.1.

Time	Group A	Group B	Group C
15 minutes	Introductory activity	Introductory activity	Introductory activity
15 minutes	Small-group meeting with teacher	Game or puzzle	Independent work
15 minutes	Independent work	Small-group meeting with teacher	Game or puzzle
15 minutes	Game or puzzle	Independent work	Small-group meeting with teacher

Figure 2.1 Possible instructional cycle

While such a schedule can be a useful format, it is only one way to include games and puzzles in our classrooms and one way to meet individual needs. If we are to use games and puzzles to develop conceptual understanding as well as to build fluency, we must reevaluate how we are using them and be willing to make some changes in our classroom instruction.

) The Purposes of Games Change over Time

The same game or puzzle can serve many different purposes, and those purposes change with increased exposure. As summarized in Figure 2.2, we view the *introduction* stage as an experience that exposes students to different ways of thinking and piques their interest. This introduction often may be the focus of the day's lesson. Students have several opportunities for follow-up play in teams, beginning within the initial lesson, during the *exploration* stage. Through this exploration, students' learning deepens, and some generalizations are formed. Students are actively involved with initial large-group discussions and engage in conversations with peers throughout this stage. During the *variation* stage, changes in the game allow for greater challenge, and as a result, the interest level in the game and its appropriateness for learning are maintained for a longer period of time. Frequent play or puzzling may be at a practice level, rather than intended for the development of ideas. This *practice* stage supports automaticity when such reinforcement is needed and is preferred by students over a typical worksheet. At this stage, learners are more likely to be working alone or playing against a single opponent. Sometimes games continue to be played as favorites, long after they have met the goal of supporting the development of conceptual understanding or computational fluency. When this *recreation* stage is reached, we encourage you to make the game an indoor recess option or have students play it at home for enjoyment, allowing your class to investigate other mathematical concepts in the limited instructional time available.

INTRODUCTION Large-group exposure to engage learners in new ideas → EXPLORATION Team playing or solving to explore ideas and create conversations → VARIATION Games or puzzles are varied to support continued learning → PRACTICE Practice to increase automaticity, perhaps alone or with a single opponent → RECREATION Frequent initial exposure leads to recreational experience

Figure 2.2 Stages of opportunities to play or solve the same game or puzzle

Setting Expectations and Sharing Responsibilities with Students

Some teachers view the setting of expectations and the sharing of responsibilities as separate topics, but we see them as intertwined. Students cannot be responsible without a clear understanding of what is expected of them. This is particularly important when the purposes of playing or solving include opportunities to develop conceptual understanding. Consider the following reflection from a fifth-grade teacher who uses games and puzzles in a different way than what his students experienced before entering this classroom. He believes strongly that students need to be accountable for learning.

TEACHER REFLECTION

In the beginning of the school year my students didn't seem to understand that games and puzzles were not just for fun, or just for practice. I gave them an introduction to a game and provided goals, directions, and ways in which they should work together while they were playing. They seemed to be willing to play the game but were very casual about how invested they were in understanding what they were learning. Some of the students spent more time arguing about whether or not to allow a roll of a die that landed on the floor than they spent discussing the mathematical ideas in the game.

Most of my students were pretty competitive about wanting to win but didn't think as much as they should have about how the strategies for winning relied upon their understanding of the math involved in the game. The tide seemed to turn when students realized that I was going to hold them accountable for what they had learned as a result of playing the game. We would come together as a class and discuss various game-winning strategies, how the math they had learned while playing the game could help them in other situations, and the conversations they'd had about math in their game groups. Over time, I saw progress in what they wrote about on the exit cards I gave them after they had played a game. Sometimes we talked about what they had written and they were able to extend their learning even further. The level of seriousness about what they were learning and their investment in being an integral part of the game playing increased significantly. It is a pleasure to join my students as they play games now; they concentrate and commit to the task. They talk about math a lot more and they know that what they are doing has value.

We believe that such a change in student conduct depends on teachers holding students accountable. We also think students need explicit access to what the expectations are and, ideally, need to share in identifying them. Further, students should have a variety of opportunities to learn ways to demonstrate positive behavior related to games and puzzles.

⟩ Protocols

Working with students to create game and/or puzzle protocols, rules, or norms they should all follow when playing or solving helps establish and clarify expectations. Such protocols should be posted in the classroom, where they are visible to all, and be referenced before, during, and after gaming and puzzling.

In one classroom a teacher asked her students, "Why do we play math games?" They all agreed that games are fun, and the teacher was pleased to hear the response "They help us learn." She gave the students the task of creating a protocol for playing math games and prompted their thinking by recording the heading *When playing math games, we should:* on chart paper. The list the students created is shown in Figure 2.3.

) Etiquette

Your students may be familiar with online etiquette; for instance, they may know not to type in all caps because that is considered screaming. They also have ideas as to how to treat one another respectfully in the classroom community. But along with a protocol, it can be helpful to discuss specific situations that arise in relation to playing and solving, particularly when doing so in teams.

When playing math games, we should:

Agree on the math that we are learning

Help each other learn the math while playing

Argue about the math, *not* about whose turn it is

Keep our materials as neat as possible

Write down our thinking on our recording sheets

Shake hands at the end of a game to show good sportsmanship

Have fun!!!

Figure 2.3 Math games protocol

One teacher asked us about ways to help her students apply expectations for "classroom citizens" to game and puzzle situations. We suggested she explore questions posed to a hypothetical "game-and-puzzle etiquette expert" and talked about how we could create scenarios for her students to consider. She agreed to try this technique with her students.

She had the students sit in a horseshoe arrangement and had teams of six students randomly choose one of the cards shown in Figure 2.4, which she had spread out face-down. (A copy of these cards can also be found on page A-3.) She told them that they had been hired as game-and-puzzle manners experts and their job was to discuss the concern, create a response to the writer's dilemma, and identify one "expert" in their group who would share it with the class. After listening to each etiquette expert's response, the whole group discussed the suggestion for how the individual could make the situation better and talked about how other approaches could help, too. They dramatized one of the scenarios and showed how it might be different if a classmate intervened. Sometimes the class made a list of ideas. For example, the students listed the following suggestions for what a student could do if a friend asked her to play a game but it was not a good choice for her: remember that you need to learn; suggest doing something else later; and be clear that it's a math choice, not about your friendship. The teacher removed the cards the groups discussed that day and planned to have the class consider other examples in a couple of weeks. Later in the year, she would have them reconsider all of the scenarios and etiquette suggestions.

Dear Etiquette Expert, Yesterday my good friend wanted to play a math game with me, but I knew it wouldn't help me learn. I didn't want to hurt her feelings, so I just played it. How could I have turned her down without hurting our friendship?	Dear Etiquette Expert, Whenever W.D. is on my team, he takes over. We are supposed to work together, but he never gives me a chance. He basically solves the puzzle all by himself. How can I keep him from doing this without looking like I am just whining?
Dear Etiquette Expert, Sometimes my partner gets really upset when we lose. She throws down the cards or dice and stomps off. Or sometimes she calls the other team names and says the game is boring. How can I help her to not be a sore loser?	Dear Etiquette Expert, I am a very shy person and get nervous when we have to form partners. I go sharpen a pencil or something. So usually I just end up with whoever is left. I don't even know how to get a partner. How can you help me?
Dear Etiquette Expert, My partner and I were working on a puzzle, but she just gave up. She said it was too hard and we shouldn't even bother to solve it. I thought we could solve it if we worked together. How can I convince her to work longer and that the effort is worth it?	Dear Etiquette Expert, My team doesn't clean up right. They just throw things in the box without sorting them. Sometimes important game pieces are left on the floor. I am getting tired of being the one to always put everything away correctly. What should I do?
Dear Etiquette Expert, Sometimes I really need to solve a puzzle alone. I get too distracted in the group and can't think about the math. I think my teacher might let me if I asked, but I'm worried about looking so different from everyone else. What do you think?	Dear Etiquette Expert, Yesterday my partner took a really long time. He had some good ideas, but it took forever for us to finish our turn because he wanted to check every possibility. How can we get the other team to be more patient and get my partner willing to stop?
Dear Etiquette Expert, The team we were playing against today made an error. I mentioned it and my partner said they should lose their turn. They got mad at me and said I wasn't the teacher and should just let it go. What do you suggest?	Dear Etiquette Expert, My team won today, but I was embarrassed by the big deal my partner made when we scored the final point. He kept telling the other team that we were much better than they were. What can I do if this happens again?
Dear Etiquette Expert, I'm not sure how to disagree with my partner when I think she is wrong, so sometimes I just agree with her. I don't want her to think I don't like her, but I want to talk more about our different ideas. What should I do?	Dear Etiquette Expert, My partner and I had a lot of questions about the puzzle today. We read the directions again, but it didn't help and everyone else looked busy. We finally just filled in some numbers and said we were done. What do you think we should have done instead?

Figure 2.4 Etiquette expert cards

) Rules Students Can Decide for Themselves

You may have had the experience of playing a particular game with new friends or with relatives who live in a different part of the country and discovering that you play the game by slightly different rules. A game of checkers may begin with players establishing whether or not you have to jump, if you can. It matters that the players agree, but either way, the game is still checkers. One teacher, who has shared this example with his students, replies, "Oh, that's a do-I-have-to-jump question that you decide for yourselves," when players ask questions such as the following:

> How do we decide who goes first?
> Does a team that makes an error lose a turn or just get corrected?
> Does a roll of the dice count if it rolls off the rug?
> Should both teams have the same number of turns, or does the game stop as soon as a team wins?

You'll find that directions to the games in this book that involve taking turns assume that players will decide who plays or takes a particular role first. When applicable, they indicate when it is a disadvantage to go first. We found that students usually relied on rolling a die if one was already needed for the game or on rock–paper–scissors when a die was not needed for play. When we asked students how they might decide, these were the two techniques they usually shared first. Students also frequently suggested using comparisons about themselves, such as closest birthday, oldest or youngest, name with the most letters, or first name in alphabetical order. One student offered, "Oh, I usually say, 'Whoever wants to be more mature today can let the other person or team go first.'" Players seem to have strong feelings about this decision, so we let them decide. You may want to have a conversation with your students and have them make a list of ways they could decide who will go first.

) Responsibility: Let Them Be the Mathematicians

As teachers, we all feel responsible for helping our students learn, but when we don't share that responsibility with them, our own behaviors could interfere unknowingly. Sometimes we might get excited when we notice a particularly good possible move in a game and point it out. Occasionally, we might draw solvers' attention to how two clues could be combined to yield important information about a puzzle. During discussions, we might answer questions to which other students could respond. All of these behaviors have the unintended consequences of limiting our students' sense of responsibility for their own learning and their development of the habits of mathematicians. We might want to ask ourselves:

> Do I do too much telling?
> Do I believe struggle can be productive and let my students struggle long enough?
> Do I have shared goals and expectations with each of my students?

No matter how long we have been teaching, we all need to ask ourselves these questions. As mentioned earlier, we encouraged students to be critics and co-creators during this writing. It wasn't long before we asked ourselves why we hadn't previously engaged students in such thinking. As we realized how much mathematical thinking we were doing as we created or adapted games, puzzles, and exit cards, we were even more amazed by this omission. Being in the role of game, puzzle, or exit card creator provides students with opportunities to analyze key ideas as well as build on and critically analyze the thinking of others, important mathematical habits of mind. So we learned, once again, that we must make sure we are offering students every opportunity to take on responsibility for their own learning. We continue to refer to this idea in each of the following sections of the chapter.

Assessing Learning and Setting Goals

Worthwhile assessment requires teachers to have a clear understanding of what is to be learned, the developmental progression in which the learning is likely to occur, and the evidence that would suggest such learning was accomplished. It is upon such a foundation that we make decisions as to how particular games and puzzles can accomplish established goals. Establishing such goals and making them clear to all stakeholders is essential.

) Setting Goals

Teachers, coaches, and administrators spend a great deal of time reviewing data and establishing learning goals. Such goal setting might be at a district, school, classroom, or student level. Shared ownership of such goals is necessary for their success and, yet, students are not always included. Rich Newman (2012) contrasts his son's ability to articulate goals related to his favorite video game with students' understanding of their learning goals in school. His son could identify goals for his playing and what he must accomplish to meet those goals. He could name recent improvements he had made and how they came about, as well as the next steps he would take to continue growth. He knew his current level of achievement, what he was best at, and specific aspects of the game he found challenging. How many of our students could give such detailed insight into their learning at school?

Some classrooms do have established practices for creating goals and involve students in that process. Consider this example from a fourth-grade classroom. Within the structure for setting goals in this classroom, students understand that the games and puzzles they are assigned to or choose to play will be aligned to their learning goals.

The students have completed a practice unit test. The teacher has given them a list of the correct responses and a rubric for evaluating the open-ended response question. In partners, students are to apply the rubric and then they are to reflect privately on two questions: What do you think you know well and why do you think so? and What do you need to work further on and why do you think so? Olivia is reviewing her thoughts with her teacher, who concurs with Olivia's report that she knows her multiplication facts up to 5 × 5 and those with 9 as one of the factors, but that she isn't always accurate when one of the factors is 6, 7, or 8. Together, they set two goals for Olivia: to rely on facts she knows to find unknown facts and to practice the facts she does not know. Together, Olivia and her teacher decide that six weeks is a reasonable time limit for meeting these goals and that they will meet weekly to check on progress. Olivia records these in her math journal, beginning with the phrase In the next six weeks I will. *She understands that these goals provide an important focus for her learning and that she will be able to measure her growth over the six weeks.*

❭ Examining the Evidence of Learning

Once learning goals are established, we collect evidence as to whether or not students are meeting them. There are a variety of assessment artifacts connected to games and puzzles, but they are not always observed, recorded, or analyzed, and we all know that teachers can't be everywhere or consider every piece of student work. That said, we believe there are ways to make such evidence more visible and thus be more readily available to inform our instructional decision making. The process begins with the initial introduction of the game or puzzle.

Observations

As soon as students begin to solve or play, we encourage you to take your clipboard or tablet and become an active observer. In your first observation you want to make sure everyone understands expectations and you want to look for trends or patterns among the students. We suggest specific observations within the "What to Look For" section for each game or puzzle, but, in general, there are four major goals for this initial observation:

❭ Make sure students are following directions correctly, and intercede as necessary, before misinterpretations are practiced and become more difficult to change.

❭ Note what students are talking about and how they are relying on one another to reach success. What vocabulary do they use? What questions do they ask one another?

❭ Look for examples you want to share during the large-group debriefing regarding partial understandings, strategies, or interactions. Prior to the debriefing, ask students' permission to share and note the order in which you want them to do so.

❭ Look for any challenging situations in which the students are having difficulty getting along while playing a game or solving a puzzle. Sometimes you may wish to address such a situation immediately, while at other times you may prefer to wait. If waiting seems best, you may want to create a related etiquette card to discuss at a later time.

Consider this teacher's reflection on what she learned by observing her students:

TEACHER REFLECTION

I introduced the Number Is/Which Number Is? *puzzle (see page 30) today. I described how the question on one card connected with the answer on another card, with the goal of having the last card match with the first one. I then gave each team of four students a set of sixteen cards. I was fascinated with the ways student teams discussed how they would start the puzzle. One group decided that the members would each answer each question together, agree, and then find the matching card. In another group, each student took four cards and worked independently, before trying to connect all of the cards. When individual answers were shared and there was no matching card, they worked together as a team. As I moved from group to group, I found that all of the early conversations were about how they would work together toward a common goal. It became clear that my students were learning important lessons about working in groups, an important life goal.*

As opportunities to play and solve continue, perhaps with variations included, you can focus on one or two groups per session to observe more carefully, taking notes regarding evidence of learning and examples of challenges for individual students.

Student Work

We suggest utilizing two sources of written work: recording sheets and responses to exit cards. Teachers found they could skim these pieces, looking for correctness or patterns among the group. Sometimes they focused on a particular student's learning, so his or her responses received more attention. For example, Figure 2.5 shows a recording sheet from the game *Think Remainder* (page 81).

What can it tell you about this student's thinking? What feedback would you give, or what question might you ask the student? Would you be more likely to direct the student's attention to $47 \div 1 = 1$ or to ask if he or she could spot an error? Note that on the next to the last line, the student recorded $23 \div 2 = 11\frac{1}{2}$. (Representing remainders as fractions had never been discussed in this class.) Through either face-to-face or writ-

Think Remainder **Recorder Sheet**

Name: _____   Date: _____

I Rolled	Number Crossed Out	Related Facts	Remainder
6	18	$6 \times 3 = 18$	0
2	24	$12 \times 2 = 24$	0
1	47	$47 \div 1 = 1$	0
3	15	$5 \times 3 = 15$	0
5	35	$5 \times 7 = 35$	0
1	44	$1 \times 44 = 44$	0
3	42	$42 \div 3 = 14$	0
2	23	$23 \div 2 = 11\frac{1}{2}$ R1	1
5	11	$2 \times 5 = 10$ R1	1

Total Score _____

Figure 2.5 One student's *Think Remainder* recording sheet

ten follow-up, a teacher may want to ask how the student arrived at a remainder of 1 with an answer of 11½. Simply asking this student to explain his or her thinking about 11½ would give the teacher and the student another opportunity to engage in a mathematical conversation.

At the end of the day, a teacher may have a pile of recording sheets and wonder what to do with them. Students often do not receive feedback about such work and often regard recording sheets as just a place to "do their math" while they are playing the game. One teacher told us, "I like to respond to the recording sheets occasionally, so students know these are more than scrap paper and that they are expected to always show their best thinking." We agree. When teachers provide feedback, students value the recording sheet more; they view it as a tool for communicating their thinking and demonstrating what they know.

There are a variety of ways you can use the exit card questions suggested in the game chapters:

❯ Use the two or three questions over time, choosing a different one each time students investigate a game or puzzle, or pose them all at once.

❯ Choose one question to give to the whole class, or vary the questions for different students based on their readiness or choices.

❯ Include one of the questions on an at-home assignment or formal assessment, letting students and parents or guardians know that games and puzzles are an integral part of their learning and require accountability.

❯ Offer one question twice, once after the first exposure to the game or puzzle and then again after further explorations, to document any changes. You may want to have students compare their two responses and reflect upon how much they have learned.

In response to both exit cards and recording sheets, you could do one of the following:

❯ Choose examples to share with students during the next math lesson.

❯ Sort responses quickly into three piles—not proficient; working toward proficiency; and proficient—and use the results to differentiate instruction.

❯ Share a simple, generic rubric (see, for example, Figure 2.6) to help clarify expectations, after which you or your students could apply it occasionally to their responses.

❯ Create a task-specific rubric with a colleague at your grade level and work together to apply it to students' responses.

❯ After reviewing them with students, place two responses to the same question or task, completed over time, in the students' portfolios to share with parents or guardians.

Student Name:		Date:	
	Novice	Developing	Strong
Concepts	There is no evidence of conceptual thinking, or thinking is incorrect.	Partial understanding of concepts is demonstrated.	Full understanding of concepts is demonstrated.
Skills	There are several computational errors.	Most computation is correct.	All computation is correct.
Communication	There is no use or mostly incorrect application of mathematical terms and symbols.	Mathematical symbols are used correctly and some relevant vocabulary is included and used correctly.	All relevant mathematical symbols and vocabulary are included and used correctly.
Communication	No or only incorrect examples or explanations are provided.	An incomplete explanation is provided, or more clarity is needed.	Explanation is clear, correct, and includes examples.

Figure 2.6 Generic rubric for exit questions and recording sheets

Fostering Productive Discussions

Math talk is now a common term, illustrating the expectation for communication in today's math classrooms. *Accountable talk* describes the specific kind of discourse in which we want our students to participate. Such talk requires students to ask each other about their thinking, listen to each other carefully, build on the ideas of others, and use evidence to justify their ideas. It also means creating classrooms where students are willing to share their initial thinking, not just their finished products. We want to build classroom communities where errors are viewed as part of the learning process, because using errors for instructional purposes has the potential to increase students' understanding (Bray 2013). Such instructional opportunities are dependent on finding tasks that allow us to tap into potential misunderstandings and creating classrooms where errors are acknowledged and valued.

To some extent, such conversations, along with the teacher talk moves suggested by Chapin, O'Connor, and Anderson (2009) and Kazemi and Hintz (2014), are incorporated into many classrooms. Our task here is to think about connecting this talk to games and puzzles.

First and foremost, such conversations depend on significant tasks. Engaging games and puzzles provide something for students to talk about. Whole-group debriefing sessions offer opportunities for students to describe the mathematical understanding they gained from the game or puzzle, discuss strategies, and explain solutions. We want students to hold these same types of conversations while they are playing and solving in small groups. Sentence frames can be used to help students participate. Examples are shown in Figure 2.7.

Ask questions when you don't understand.	Can you explain why this move …? What do you mean when you say that …? Can you help me to …?
Ask about the thinking of others.	What do you think we should …? How did you decide …? Do you want to say anything about …?
Make predictions.	I predict that … If we do …, then I think …
Build on the thinking of others.	I agree with …, but … I use this idea, too, when I play, but I … _____'s idea makes me think …
Give and ask for evidence of thinking.	An example from the game we played is … I think … because … Can you tell me why it is true that …?
Look for patterns and generalizations.	Now I am wondering … This puzzle reminds me of … We could also use this when playing …

Figure 2.7 Sentence frames for games and puzzles

Meeting Individual Differences

Your assessment data will help you identify mathematical readiness levels. Several specific ways to meet such differences are suggested in the game chapters within the "Variations" sections. Ideas for meeting other differences are provided in the "Tips from the Classroom" sections. Here we would like to provide a general list of ideas.

- With permission, create a video of students playing the game that other students may watch as a way to see the directions in action. This can be particularly helpful for students who learn best by example, rather than oral or written directions.
- Create sound barriers for rolling dice by having students use rug samples, sometimes available for free at carpet stores, or appropriately sized boxes lined with felt.
- Cards and dice come in a variety of sizes, colors, and textures. Offering a variety allows students to choose what's best for them.
- Create an area to play and solve that is somewhat private, perhaps behind a bookcase, as an option for students who will have better success when working in an area that is less distracting.
- Some students may not have time to complete an exit card during class. Sometimes you may wish to collect whatever those students have completed. Other times, you or they could choose to include completing or refining responses in their homework.
- As students play and solve together, some may prefer to respond to exit cards together as well. You can vary expectations for cooperative and individual responses.

> Allow some students to help create answers for recording sheets and responses to exit cards while relying on their partners for the actual recording.

> Students react in different ways to competitive play. Though it can be motivating for many, some become overly competitive and others resist competition or become quite anxious. Nearly all games can be played cooperatively, with the goal of trying to improve by working together.

> Some students may not have the fine-motor abilities to shuffle cards. Show them how cards can be cut and rearranged several times or spread out on a flat surface and moved around before re-forming a deck.

Organizing Students for Success

After many years of thinking that the best way to introduce a new game or puzzle format was to demonstrate it for a few students and then let them introduce it to others, we now believe that a new game or puzzle format should be introduced by the teacher to the whole class or a large instructional group. You'll find that each of the games and puzzles in this book are introduced in this manner. This does not mean that you always have to play an entire game or completely solve a puzzle in a large-group setting. Sometimes you can consider a miniature version of the game or puzzle, just take a few turns or look at a few puzzle clues as a class, or explore or review related mathematics and relevant terms. We believe such introductory experiences help students in the following ways:

> They support the notion that students are part of a diverse learning community.

> They model and reinforce expectations for how best to play games or solve puzzles with team members, be patient with opponents, persevere, and be gracious winners and losers.

> They model and reinforce ways to participate in accountable talk related to games and puzzles.

> They increase the likelihood that students will be able to follow directions and meet expectations during opportunities to play or solve.

> They provide you with opportunities to gain the formative assessment data you need to differentiate follow-up opportunities for students to play the game or solve similar puzzles.

) Grouping Students

When games and puzzles are just for practice, teachers often group students homogeneously and have one student compete against another or have students complete a puzzle alone. When the goal is to build a deeper understanding of mathematics and mathematical habits of mind or practices, heterogeneous grouping makes more sense. As Wedekind states, "The idea of grouping kids by ability level is counterproductive to the idea that mathematicians learn from each other" (2011, 30). Playing games and doing puzzles can provide wonderful opportunities for students with different abilities to discuss a common goal. Students may be surprised to find that classmates who they thought were struggling with a concept have interesting strategies to offer or connect clues that others hadn't thought to try. Thinking of all students in the room as mathematicians, rather than just those students who seem to be the fastest and most verbal about what they know, brings new light to learning opportunities.

As with all classroom activities, you always have the choice to assign students to teams, pick opposing teams, and select locations for play, or you may choose to have the students make such decisions independently. Though we support having students make such decisions whenever possible, we often lean toward having the teacher make these decisions when the class is first considering a new game or puzzle format, assigning students in ways that will support students' learning. You can display the information for all to see so that little time is lost in finding co-players and locations. If the schedule allows, we recommend that students play or solve, in teams, immediately after they have experienced a whole-class introduction.

❭ Having Students Play and Solve in Teams

When the goal of playing a game or solving a puzzle is to deepen learning, rather than only to practice skills, we recommend having students play and solve in teams rather than as individual players. While we recognize that for a few students this may be too challenging, we consider it optimal in nearly all cases. Sometimes, particularly with puzzles, students need a few minutes to work independently before teaming, and this is fine. We've found that some students prefer to read independently and try to interpret a clue or two by themselves but then, without prompting, begin to work with their partners. Some teachers build in independent think time before cooperative thinking, and some groups build this in for themselves. We remember Jason, who suggested to his group, "Let's read first and then we can talk."

Some teachers organize teams before introducing a game or puzzle; others draft team combinations, perhaps by using magnetized name cards on a cookie sheet, that can be quickly altered based on assessment data gathered during the introductory experience. Other teachers prefer to quickly organize teams with oral directions, and some allow students to organize themselves. Regardless of how teams were organized, we have been privy to wonderfully unique and informative mathematical conversations by listening to students play and solve in teams. Consider the following reflection from one of the teachers who worked with us.

TEACHER REFLECTION

Traditionally the kids in my class would play games against a partner. They didn't want to talk about the math because they didn't want to give away their strategies, especially when there was strong competition. I was surprised by the impact of having students play in team pairs. Immediately the noise level in my room increased in a good way. The students needed to talk about their strategies with their partners and they would debate about which strategy was best. I also found that kids who didn't have strategies benefited from their partners' think-alouds, and over time, they began to try out the same strategies on their own.

⟩ Regaining Students' Attention

The engagement of a good game or puzzle can lead to a higher level of noise in the classroom than some teachers would prefer. No doubt you have one or more signals that remind students to use their inside voices or alert them to immediately stop and pay attention to you. Many teachers find that ringing a chime or striking a triangle works well. When you introduce such a system, likely during the first week of school, it is important that students practice the expected response while playing a game or engaging in solving a puzzle. Interrupting such activities may be challenging for them, especially if they feel as if they are about to win or reach a collaborative goal or solution. Assuring students that they can return to the game or puzzle after you have finished talking or at another time will often facilitate this process.

⟩ Making Directions Accessible

Frequent requests to repeat or provide another copy of directions can be frustrating. As you know, this is not a good use of your time, nor does it teach students to listen, remember, or organize their own materials. To avoid these distractions, you could

⟩ establish an area in the room where directions are available (A reproducible with directions is provided for each game or puzzle in this book.);

⟩ videotape yourself reading the directions and make the video available on the classroom website or available for showing at a designated area in the classroom; or

⟩ encourage students to write a short, personalized version of the directions they can keep with them while they are playing the game for the first time.

Organizing Materials for Success

Puzzles often do not require materials, but games usually do. A designated area of well-organized materials makes it more likely that students will respect and return game components appropriately. Sending a classroom of students to play or solve in groups requires multiple copies of materials and containers. This does not mean that schools or teachers need to spend a great deal of money. Attics, basements, garage sales, families, and websites like the Freecycle Network (http://www.freecycle.org/), have much to offer, such as baskets, cookie tins, egg cartons, muffin tins, oatmeal boxes, plastic containers, shoeboxes, soap cases, and silverware organizers. What you use depends, of course, on the space and materials available to you; boxes, zip-top bags, pocket charts, and file folders are among some of the other possibilities.

If your materials are well cared for and organized, it sends a message that playing games is important and that you trust students enough to let them use materials that are attractive. Here are some questions and responses that can guide your thinking about the organization of game materials in your classroom.

> *Does the organization and labeling encourage student independence?* Clear labels on containers that are organized in a systematic way allow students to find and return materials more easily. Game directions along with a list of materials pasted inside each game container help ensure that components won't get lost and help students meet expectations for play and for cleaning up.

> *Does the organization support long-term game use?* Placing number cards in a soap dish within a box protects the cards, as does laminating any paper materials.

> *Does the organization support large-group use?* Large-group instruction requires multiple copies of materials. Keep multiple sets together in easily carried containers when preparing to introduce a new game. Some of these copies can then be moved to the game library for students to sign out to take home.

> *Does the organization maximize instructional time?* Having extra sets of frequently needed materials, such as dice or cards, allows students to replace missing components immediately, when needed. Same-size containers stack easily, and allow games to be put away more quickly.

Working with Families

We know that the amount of parent involvement correlates to student achievement; this also applies to games and puzzles (Kliman 2006). Involving families in game playing or solving a puzzle gives both students and family members the opportunity to share the math together in a way that is different than completing a worksheet or doing problems from a textbook. Playing a game with a sibling, older or younger, allows the student to take a leadership role in explaining the rules and sharing what he or she has learned about the game or puzzle and the mathematics involved. The conversation about the math they are learning is embedded in a meaningful context, and parents are likely to gain more information than they get in response to the question *What did you do in school today?*

One way to let parents understand the importance of playing the games or doing the puzzles with their children is to offer a games-and-puzzles party. You could invite family members to an afternoon or evening event in which you explain the directions to a game just as you would to students. Often, parents are not aware of the academic language we are using in schools to talk about mathematics. Highlighting math vocabulary for parents can positively affect how they communicate about math with their children. Then parents and their children can sit together to play the game, perhaps with simple refreshments provided. Alternatively, the students could explain the game to their families in small groups. Parents have been known to share their understanding of the math and how it is different from the way they learned it. The opportunity to address such issues and help parents understand current practices is essential, as parents identify this difference as a barrier to their involvement (Brock and Edmunds 2011). You could also invite families to bring in a favorite math-related game from their home or country of origin to share with another group.

Some families may be surprised that their children are playing games in class. You can communicate why the use of games and puzzles is important in a classroom through an email message or a letter, perhaps including the directions for a popular game or the questions that students must answer on an exit card after

---

Dear parent(s) or guardian(s),

Your child will work hard this year to understand the mathematics he or she is learning, compute efficiently, and be a strong problem solver. Many times we will use games and puzzles to support this learning. Students will play and solve in groups so they can talk about their thinking and discuss their strategies. I use exit cards (short questions students answer after playing a game or solving a puzzle) and recording sheets to make sure the students are recording what they are learning while they are playing or solving. Your child may bring home a puzzle or game to share with you, and I hope you will enjoy exploring it with him or her. As a result of these activities, your child will recall basic facts quickly, gain number sense, and become a stronger mathematician.

To give you a better idea of the types of games and puzzles we will be using, I am sending along …

Figure 2.8 Sample note to parents and guardians

completing a puzzle. A sample of an introduction to such a note is provided in Figure 2.8. The more family members understand about the value of games and puzzles, the more willing they will be to spend time exploring them at home.

You can establish a lending library in your classroom, allowing students to bring home games and take responsibility for doing so. One method for providing structure to this responsibility is to include a materials list with each game packet that must be checked off when the game is returned. Students can check out the game from the classroom games library just as they would a library book, writing their name on an index card and placing it in a file or container designated for this purpose. Include a comment card in the bag so that students and their families can write something about an interesting conversation they had, something new they learned, or questions they had while they were playing. This card could be shared with the next families who explore the game.

You can also require students to play a game or solve a puzzle as part of their homework. Require students to record the work of a family member while playing the game or describe a challenge a sibling encountered when solving a puzzle. Encouraging written communication about what transpired at home will provide students with an opportunity to solidify their thinking about the mathematics content.

Conclusion

We know you recognize that the instructional practices addressed in this chapter relate to all aspects of your teaching, but we hope that you can now envision them more distinctly in game- and puzzle-related situations. We also hope that you'll discover new joy in using these games and puzzles or some of your old favorites with these ideas in mind. Your students will appreciate the opportunities to learn in this manner and you will see growth in their mathematical understanding and their computational fluency.

Base Ten Numeration

What's the Math?

Numbers permeate our lives. And as technology allows us to access real-world numerical data instantly, number sense is essential to making good decisions both in and out of the classroom. Noncomputational ideas related to number sense include making connections among different representations of numbers such as quantities, word names, and symbols; understanding differences in the magnitude of numbers, for example, how much greater one thousand is than one hundred; and understanding how our number system works. Students should know, for instance, that the difference between $350 and $3,500 is more significant that just adding another 0.

Counting and our base ten number system are fundamental ideas of mathematics, but unfortunately, ideas related to place value can be difficult to teach and to learn (Ross 2002). Among students with learning challenges, a common difficulty is the idea that ten ones can form a new unit that is one ten (Thouless 2014), a concept key to several computational strategies, including standard algorithms.

Students need many opportunities to explore numbers in flexible ways in order to recognize the many forms in which numbers can be expressed and still be equivalent—for example, to know that 39 tens is equivalent to 390 ones. Though manipulatives are considered necessary, but not sufficient (McNeil and Jarvin 2007), students should have ample time to explore models such as number lines, number charts, and base ten manipulatives and to gain a sense of which visual models best apply to particular situations.

The games and puzzles provided here engage students in these fundamental ideas and allow concepts related to number and place value to deepen. Some of the games and puzzles connect to addition and subtraction, though number and base ten numeration are always the main focus. For instance, finding a number 200 more than 5,000 can be thought of as an addition example, or as merely placing a 2 in the hundreds place of 5,000, a place-value concept.

Which Number Is Closest?

Why This Game or Puzzle?

Much instructional attention is given to the ten-to-one (moving left) and one-to-ten (moving right) place-value relationships within our base ten number system. These concepts are essential to understanding traditional computational algorithms. Sometimes the focus on regrouping can overshadow other important place-value ideas critical to number sense. Mathematics instruction that focuses on the magnitude of numbers has a positive impact on student learning (Faulkner 2009).

The *Which Number Is Closest?* game board presents five goal numbers, with spaces to write eighteen digits for forming numbers as close to the goal numbers as possible. The game leader draws a card from two sets of number cards labeled 0–9 that have been shuffled together. The student reads the number on the card, and players write it in one of the open digit spaces on their game boards. Play continues until all digit spaces are filled. (Note that two cards will not be used.) Players then compare the numbers they formed with the goal numbers. Students are often quite surprised at what a difference the placement of the digits makes.

Which Number Is Closest? Game Board

Name(s): _____ Date: _____

Goal Number	Number Created
100	☐☐☐
1,000	☐☐☐☐
500	☐☐☐
1,000	☐☐☐

Math Focus

› Comparing numbers
› Forming numbers close to given numbers

Materials Needed

› 1 *Which Number Is Closest?* Game Board per team (page A-4)
› 1 deck of *Which Number Is Closest?* Cards (made from *two* copies of page A-5) per group of players
› Optional: 1 *Which Number Is Closest?* Directions per group (page A-6)

Directions

Goal: Place digits in the spaces to form numbers as close in value as possible to the goal numbers.

› Shuffle the cards and place them facedown. Choose a player to be the game leader.
› The game leader turns over one card and announces the number. Each team writes the digit in one of the spaces (boxes) in the "Number Created" column of the game board.
› All teams must record the digit before the next number is announced, and once written, its placement may not be changed.
› The leader continues turning over cards until eighteen digits have been placed. (Note that the last two cards will not be used.)
› Compare how close each of the teams' numbers is to each goal number. The team with the closest number wins a point. Each team adds its points to find its score. The team with the most points wins the game.

How It Looks in the Classroom

One third-grade teacher begins by saying, "Turn and talk to your neighbor about what numbers you think are close to 500." After a minute of talk time, she asks the students to share their thinking and records their answers on a sheet of chart paper. Their responses include numbers in the early 500s; 490–510; numbers that round to 500; 499 and 501; and numbers just less or just more than 500.

She then gives each student a copy of the game board on page A-4 and tells them to find their names on the lists she has projected and seat themselves accordingly. (She has listed students' names in groups of four, with partner pairs identified in each group.) Once the partnerships are formed, she asks the students in each pair to share one game board and save the second copy for another game. She explains the rules of the game, which are listed on chart paper, and tells them that partners should talk together before writing each digit on their shared board. She tells them that they'll start with a practice game, and then she randomly draws a number card and reads the first digit for them to write.

Later in the game, groans are heard after the teacher reads aloud the eighteenth digit; clearly several teams were hoping she would draw another 1. She has the teams determine their scores just to make sure that they know how to do so. She then has each group at a table choose a leader to get a set of cards for play and to be the one to turn them over and announce the digits. She is then free to check in with groups and make assessment notes as relevant while they play another round of the game.

Tips from the Classroom

> Students may wish to play several rounds of this game, as each time they play they learn to make better choices as to where to write the digits. Consider laminating boards or copying the game board on both sides of the paper.

> Some teams may take a long time to decide where to write a digit. Using a 30-second timer can be helpful to keep the game moving.

> Consider students' pace when determining teams. A quick or impulsive thinker paired with a slower or methodical thinker may or may not make a good partnership. You may wish to exchange partners after observing the practice round.

> As the focus of the game is on place value, you may wish to give students the option of using calculators to find the differences between their numbers and the goal numbers.

> If you have several teams playing this game at once and you have access to an application or other form of technology that can record students' conversations and/or written work, you may wish to have students use it. One teacher commented, "I can't believe the place-value conversations this game stimulates."

What to Look For

> Do players appear tentative or confident as they write the named digits?
> What base ten language do students use?
> What ideas do students talk about when deciding where to write the digits?
> Do students make sensible decisions about where they place their digits?

Variations

> After giving students a few opportunities to play in teams, you may wish to allow individual students to play against a partner.

> To make the game easier, change the last number to 100, provide only two digit places, and have players draw only fifteen of the cards.

> To increase the challenge, add decimal points to the goal numbers and their corresponding digit places.

❭ Once students are familiar with the game, change how players find their scores. Have teams find the differences between each of the goal numbers and the numbers they formed and then find the total of these differences. The team with the least sum wins. This scoring method further emphasizes the values of the digits.

Exit Card Choices

❭ If the first card were a 0, where would you place it? Why?

❭ If the first card were a 0, what would you like the second number to be, and where would you place it?

❭ How did playing this game help you to learn about place value?

Note the student work shown in Figure 3.1. Responding to the first exit question above, the student identified the best place to write the 0 but did not explain why in terms of the significant impact a greater digit in the thousands place would have, nor did the student refer to the names of the other places in the number. The teacher knew that the student knew the names of the places and wondered why the student didn't include them. She decided that she needed to point out the importance of using precise language.

> I woud put the zero in the thousands place so that I would put a one in the first place and then all small numbers in the last three places so that I would have a number highter than 10,000 but low so that I would get ō point.

Figure 3.1 Student response to first exit question

Extension

Once students have played the game with the adaptation of having their scores be the total of their differences from the goal numbers, assign the homework task, *Now that you know the possible eighteen digits, where would you place them to get the least sum?*

Game adapted from *How Close Can You Get?* in *Zeroing in on Number and Operations: Key Ideas and Common Misconceptions, Grades 3–4,* by Linda Dacey and Anne Collins (Portland, ME: Stenhouse, 2010).

The Number Is/What Number Is?

Why This Game or Puzzle?

For this puzzle, each group of students gets a copy of the set of cards on page A-7, each of which lists an answer and a question. The students must arrange the cards in a circle so that the answer to the question on one card is shown on the card that follows it. Further, all of the cards must be included in the circle.

Some questions have more than one correct response, though only one choice will allow all of the cards to be included in the solution circle. The need to work as a team, with all of the cards, leads students to engage in conversations about how best to work together, which choices to make, and what to do when some cards have been excluded from their solution.

You can adapt the clues so that they are limited to four-digit whole numbers or so they include decimals. Questions such as *What number is 17 hundreds and 15 tens?* are puzzling to many students, which gives them opportunities to build perseverance in solving problems, the first of the mathematical practices listed in the Common Core State Standards (NGA/ CCSSO 2010). These questions also provide opportunities to recognize a variety of ways to represent a number, a skill essential to fully understanding regrouping in the traditional addition and subtraction algorithms. Questions such as *What is 2,000 more than 10,000?* emphasize the power of place value because it is not necessary to add using paper and pencil to answer the question; instead, you can just increase the thousands digit by two.

(This puzzle is adapted from the game *I Have/Who Has?* Because it is a puzzle, however, students' turns are never over, and conversations are encouraged. You can use cards from preexisting *I Have/Who Has?* games for this puzzle.)

The Number Is/What Number Is? Cards

The number is 236,427. What number is 250 tens and 3 ones?	The number is 2,503. What number is 50,000 + 700 + 3?	The number is 50,703. What number is rounded to 2,500 when rounded to the nearest hundred?	The number is 2,489. What number is greater than 350 thousands?
The number is 405,786. What number is 2,000 more than 10,000?	The number is 12,000. What number is 17 hundreds and 15 tens?	The number is 1,850. What number is less than 2,000?	The number is 1,715. What number is one more than 15,699?
The number is fifteen thousand seven hundred. What number is between 10,000 and 14,000?	The number is 13,700. What number is rounded to 25,000 when rounded to the nearest thousand?	The number is 25,499. What number is 200,000 + 40,000 + 7?	The number is two hundred forty thousand seven. What number is 10,000 + 400 + 30 + 6?
The number is ten thousand four hundred thirty-six. What number is 72 hundreds?	The number is 7,200. What number is 2,000 + 500 + 60 + 3?	The number is 2,563. What number is between 70 tens and 80 tens?	The number is 742. What number is less than 800?
The number is 450. What number is 63 thousands, 25 hundreds, 18 ones?	The number is 65,518. What number is greater than half a million?	The number is 827,345. What number rounds to 20,000 when rounded to the nearest ten thousand?	The number is 18,239. What number is rounded to 200,000 when rounded to the nearest hundred thousand?

Math Focus

> Reading numbers written in words or numerals
> Rounding numbers up or down
> Comparing numbers
> Recognizing nonstandard forms of the same number

Materials Needed

> 1 deck of *The Number Is/What Number Is?* Cards per group of two to four students (page A-7)
> Optional: 1 set of *The Number Is/What Number Is?* Cards to Make Your Own Puzzle per pair of students (page A-8)
> Optional: 1 *The Number Is/What Number Is?* Directions per group (page A-9)

Directions

Goal: Place cards so that the number identified on each card answers the question on the card before it.

> Spread out the cards faceup on a table or the floor.
> Choose a card and read its question.
> Find a card with a matching answer, place this card next to the first card, and read the question on this second card.
> Continue to read questions and find answers. Organize the cards in a circle so that each question is followed with a correct answer.
> Each card must be included in the circle.

How It Looks in the Classroom

One teacher introduces the puzzle by telling students that she will show them cards that they must put in order so that each question is followed by a correct answer, eventually matching the first and last card. She then displays the mini-puzzle in Figure 3.2 on the interactive whiteboard, so she can move the "cards" as the students direct. She reads the question on card A, and Jax suggests that the number is 820. She moves card C next to card A, and Jax reads the new question at the bottom of card C.

"Wait," Aleigh proclaims. "The answer is 1,000, and that's the card we started with, but we haven't used all the cards. What do we do now?" The teacher is tempted to tell them to check the other cards, but she waits so that the students can take responsibility.

Then Ricardo says, "What about 751?" The teacher replaces card C with card D.

The class continues until the four cards are placed in order (A, D, B, C). The teacher then distributes the prepared decks of shuffled cards and says, "Remember that all twenty of the cards have to be included. If you have a card left over, you may have to change where you placed another card."

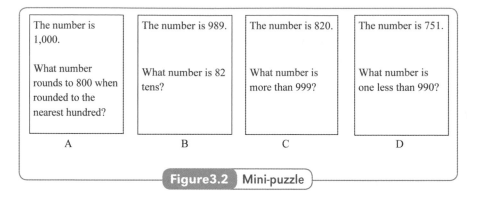

Figure3.2 Mini-puzzle

The students begin eagerly. One group finishes quite quickly, in about ten minutes. The teacher checks the group's solution and, after confirming that it is correct, has the students split into two pairs to create their own versions of the puzzle. She is startled when one of the students suggests the question *What number is four factorial?* She hadn't realized what a great opportunity this would be to differentiate learning. The group to complete the puzzle last takes about forty minutes, but the students stay focused and have some interesting conversations about how to determine the standard forms of numbers written in a nonstandard format.

Tips from the Classroom

> As with many puzzles (and real-life problems), sometimes the best thing to do is to take a break. Have students take and print a picture of their work thus far, so that they can re-create it easily.

> Some students will benefit from using a place-value chart to help them think about nonstandard representations of numbers.

> Printing the cards on sticky notes or putting magnets on their backs and having students arrange them on a metal cookie sheet may help some students organize their work more easily.

> Some students may find it easier to place the cards in a line. Just remind them that the last card must lead back to the first.

> Students can be assigned to other groups in the role of advisor or checker once they have found a correct solution. Encourage these students to ask and respond to questions rather than supplying the group with a correct answer.

What to Look For

> How do groups decide how to begin solving the puzzle?

> How do students determine equivalent representations of numbers?

> What do students do when they have yet to find a way to fit all of the cards?

Variations

❭ Add an "ask a friend" rule, which would allow students to ask a classmate working in another group for a hint or to verify whether an answer is correct.

❭ Vary the level of difficulty by challenging some students to complete the puzzle without any recording, some with use of paper and pencil, and some with access to a calculator.

❭ You can make the puzzle easier by eliminating the last row of cards and making the first card read *The number is 236* so that it will respond to the last card.

Exit Card Choices

❭ Which number did you find most challenging to identify? Why?

❭ Write two different questions for the answer 2,489.

❭ What number is 42 hundreds and 13 tens? Explain.

Extension

Have students create their own puzzles using the form on page A-8. The easiest way to do so is to start with the question on the first card and then proceed from answer to question until the end, when the answer to the last question is recorded on the first card. Once recorded in this order, any card may be chosen randomly as the first card.

Mystery Number

Why This Game or Puzzle?

Terrific for playing as a whole class during transition times, this game can also be played in small groups or pairs. The teacher or student leaders choose a number and announce, "The mystery number is between ...," and provide two endpoints, such as 500 and 1,000. The players' job is to ask questions that have yes-or-no answers until they can identify the mystery number.

The mathematics of the game focuses on comparison of numbers, most associated with a number line model, as well as other number properties, for example, the number of digits, whether it is odd or even, or whether it is a multiple of another number. The game also provides an opportunity for thinking about strategy through conversations related to the questions *What makes a good question? What can you conclude from the answers to previous questions? What's a good way to organize the information? Whether your questions are answered yes or no, how many questions do you think you'll need to ask to identify this number?* Such thinking is important, as the way mathematics is explored in classrooms should reflect how it is used in the world (Van de Walle, Karp, and Bay-Williams 2013).

As the level of the game is dependent only on the range of numbers provided and the types of questions students ask, it is appropriate for all grade levels.

Mystery Number Recording Sheet

Name(s): _____ Date: _____

The range for this game is _____ to _____

Questions Asked	What We Know Now

Math Focus

› Comparing numbers
› Identifying number word names
› Recognizing properties of numbers

Materials Needed

› 1 *Mystery Number* Recording Sheet per team (page A-10)
› Optional: 1 *Mystery Number* Directions per group of four students (page A-11)

Directions

Goal: Ask questions that can be answered with *yes* or *no* to identify the mystery number.

› Decide which team will choose the mystery number and which team will try to guess it. The team choosing the mystery number also identifies a range of numbers it is between, for example, between 500 and 800 or between 0.46 and 0.875. A player on this team privately writes down the number and range and begins the game by saying, "The mystery number is between ...," and naming the range of numbers.

› Players on the other team ask questions that can be answered only with *yes* or *no*, such as *Is the number even?* These players record questions and conclusions on the team's recording sheet.

› Questions are asked until a player identifies the answer by posing a question such as *Is the number 4.7?* and having the other team respond *yes* and share what was recorded at the beginning of the game.

How It Looks in the Classroom

One third-grade teacher begins by telling students, "You are going to be detectives, trying to identify a mystery number. Like all good detectives, you must collect evidence and take notes about the clues you find. You'll learn about the number by asking me questions that I can answer only by saying *yes* or *no.* When you think you have enough clues to identify the number, such as 754, you can ask me the question, *Is the number 754?*"

The teacher then begins the game by saying, "I am thinking of a whole number between 400 and 600."

Ralph calls out, "Is it 456?"
The teacher replies, "No. Now, think about how to record this information."
Hanis asks, "Is it less than 500?"
This time the teacher replies, "Yes."

The game continues until the number 432 is identified. The teacher has volunteers share their recordings made during the game using the document camera. Some students simply recorded the questions and answers. One student used a number line, a strategy others think is helpful. Figure 3.3 shows how the number line looked after the first two questions. Note how the student showed the original range, indicated the decreased range (though inexactly), and noted that 456 was not a candidate.

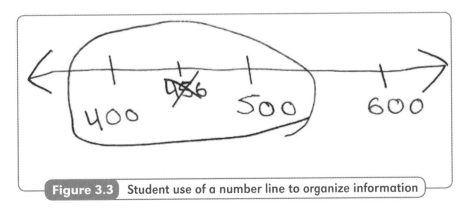

Figure 3.3 Student use of a number line to organize information

The teacher then organizes students in groups of four. She tells them, "Two students in each group will ask questions and two will answer them. After one game, change roles and play again." She then distributes recording sheets for them to use. (See page A-10.) She focuses their playing by saying, "After you play, we will talk about what makes a good question to ask."

Tips from the Classroom

) Some students will benefit from receiving a copy of a number line that shows the initial range of numbers. Such a reference can be particularly helpful for checking the correctness of leaders' responses during and after the game.

) Students could use whiteboards to record their work so they can hold them up for others to see.

) Encourage students to stop at some point in the game to reflect on their data and decide what information they want to know next.

) The assessment data gained from students' completion of the recording sheet are informative, but it is not necessary to complete such a recording for every game. As students become more familiar with the game, they may prefer to use their own recording methods.

What to Look For

) How do students organize the information they gather?

) Are students asking questions whose answers they could deduce from the answers to previous questions?

) What kinds of questions do students ask? Are their questions broad/specific enough? Do they vary their questions or focus on only one or two ideas?

) Which students need more support to recognize questions that are better than others to ask?

Variations

) Have two teams play against each other, each choosing a number and alternatively asking questions. The first team to identify the number wins.

) Encourage students to ask the fewest number of questions necessary. Note that some students may discover a problem-solving strategy called "halving the decision space." With each question, they try to eliminate half of the numbers. For example, if the range were from 0 to 1,000, the first question could be *Is it greater than 500?* If it were, the next question could be *Is it greater than 750?* One way to encourage this kind of thinking is to ask questions such as *Were you lucky that your question was answered with a yes? What would you have learned if the answer had been no? Is there a question you could ask that would be equally helpful whether the answer were either* yes *or* no?

Exit Card Choices

) A group is playing a game and the guessers have gathered the following information:

The number is between 400 and 500.

There is a 5 in the tens place.

The number is even.

It is not 456.

What numbers could the mystery number be? How do you know?

〉 The game leader has announced that the mystery number is between 0 and 1,000. What question would you ask first? Why?

Extension

Present the following scenario for students to respond to in pairs:

The game has just begun. The number is between 200 and 800. Your partner asks the question Is it 298? *What ideas could you give your partner about what questions to ask during the game? Write a note that your partner could refer to the next time he or she plays.*

Get to One or One-Tenth

Why This Game or Puzzle?

In the earlier grades we give our students many opportunities to count, to use a hundreds board, and to use manipulatives to trade ten ones for one ten. As new types of numbers are introduced, such as fractions and decimals, many students do not continue to have similar opportunities. These experiences are important, as research tells us that students are often focused on whole numbers when they compare decimal numbers. Some students may consider, for example, 0.09 to be greater than 0.1 because they know 9 is greater than 1 (Roche 2005). Here, a classic game used with whole numbers is adapted for use with decimals.

Two game boards are included for this game. One focuses on the relationships among hundredths, tenths, and ones as players roll a die, choose whether to have the number represent hundredths or tenths, and then count forward that amount. The first team to get to one, without going beyond, wins the game. When using the thousandths board, players roll to reach one-tenth.

Get to One Hundredths Game Board

0.01	0.02	0.03	0.04	0.05	0.06	0.07	0.08	0.09	0.10
0.11	0.12	0.13	0.14	0.15	0.16	0.17	0.18	0.19	0.20
0.21	0.22	0.23	0.24	0.25	0.26	0.27	0.28	0.29	0.30
0.31	0.32	0.33	0.34	0.35	0.36	0.37	0.38	0.39	0.40
0.41	0.42	0.43	0.44	0.45	0.46	0.47	0.48	0.49	0.50
0.51	0.52	0.53	0.54	0.55	0.56	0.57	0.58	0.59	0.60
0.61	0.62	0.63	0.64	0.65	0.66	0.67	0.68	0.69	0.70
0.71	0.72	0.73	0.74	0.75	0.76	0.77	0.78	0.79	0.80
0.81	0.82	0.83	0.84	0.85	0.86	0.87	0.88	0.89	0.90

Math Focus
› Counting by hundredths, tenths, and thousandths
› Recognizing the values of hundredths, tenths, and thousandths
› Reading, writing, and comparing decimals

Materials Needed
› 1 die per team
› 1 chip per team
› 1 *Get to One* Hundredths Game Board (page A-12) or *Get to One-Tenth* Thousandths Game Board per team (page A-13)
› 1 *Get to One or One-Tenth* Recording Sheet per team (page A-14)
› Optional: 1 *Get to One or One-Tenth* Directions per group (page A-15)

Directions
Goal: Move forward on the game board by tenths or hundredths (or thousandths) to reach 1.00 (or 0.1).
› Decide which team goes first.
› On each turn, a team's representative rolls the die and talks with the team about whether to have the number represent tenths or hundredths (or hundredths or thousandths). That number is then counted on the hundredths (or thousandths) board, starting at 0. Players can indicate their position by counting and placing a chip on the final number.
› Alternate turns, with each team counting on from its last number.
› If a team cannot fully complete a count, for example, the team is on 0.97 and rolls a 4, the turn is lost.
› The first team to reach 1.00 (or 0.1) wins the game.
(See alternative rules suggested by students in the "Tips from the Classroom" section.)

How It Looks in the Classroom
One fourth-grade teacher gives each team a laminated hundredths board and a chip so that the students can mark the outcomes of their team's decisions. He asks, "What do you notice about this hundredths board?" After students share several observations, he asks questions to review renaming between hundredths and tenths such as *Where would you be on the board if you started at zero and counted forward until you landed on a number equal to one-tenth?* and *What is another number name for thirty-hundredths?*

He quickly divides the class into two teams, based on where the students are sitting. He also designates a leader for each team, choosing students who he knows will confer with their teammates. The students decide the leaders will roll a die to determine which team will play first. He has the leaders roll the die on the front table, under the document camera, so that all of the students can see the outcomes. Team 1's leader, Amiti, rolls the greater number. She rolls again and the die shows six dots. She quickly returns to check with her team.

Bwan announces, "It should be tenths because that will make us more than halfway there."

Richard responds, "But maybe we should do hundredths, so we don't get stuck."

Amiti says, "Let's take a quick vote."

The group decides to move forward six-tenths. The teacher invites the current leader to choose a teammate to move the chip on the board appropriately. Teams alternate turns, and the teacher notices the students' excitement growing as both chips near 1.00. Team 1 is on 0.96 and Team 2 is on 0.93. Team 2 rolls a 6 and moves forward to 0.99. There is tension as Amiti rolls. The die lands on 4, so Team 1 chooses hundredths and wins. The students are eager to play their own games in teams composed of two players. The teacher gives them recording sheets (see page A-14) to use for one of their games so that he can learn more about their thinking.

Tips from the Classroom

❭ Some students may prefer a more tactile experience. Use base ten blocks, with the flat representing one, the longs representing tenths, and the units representing hundredths, and a place-value chart to organize the materials. Ask questions such as *How can you explain why the pieces represent the numbers that they do?*

❭ In the excitement of the game, a leader may simply accept a suggestion for choosing tenths or hundredths without checking with the team. Simply remind leaders of their roles when this happens.

What to Look For

❭ When students move forward by tenths, do they count forward ten one-hundredths for each tenth or move down one row vertically for each tenth?

❭ What mathematical understandings do students demonstrate as they decide whether to choose hundredths or tenths?

❭ What level of confidence do students exhibit when choosing the value of the number? Do they make reasonable choices? Can they explain their choices?

Variations

❭ As mentioned in Chapter 2, we think it is important to occasionally ask students how they might change the rules of a game. After playing this game, students made two interesting suggestions:

› The team that goes second should always get a last turn. Jared encouraged everyone to think about it like baseball. He explained, "You always get your last ups." All the students in Jared's class agreed to this suggestion.

> Maxine thought it would be more exciting if you could decide whether to count forward or backward on each turn. She explained, "My team might still lose, but we'd have a chance, rather than losing when we rolled something too big." There was mixed reaction to this suggestion, and the teacher decided to offer students the opportunity to play with or without this rule. But he encouraged the students to make the rules clear before they started a game.

> Students can play similarly, but start at 1.00 and count back.

> Students ready to work with thousandths can play *Get to One-Tenth*, using the game board on page A-13 and deciding whether to add thousandths or hundredths on each turn.

Exit Card Choices

> List all the ways you could win the game in two turns.

> What could you roll to get to 1.00 (or 0.1) in four turns? Write an equation to represent these moves.

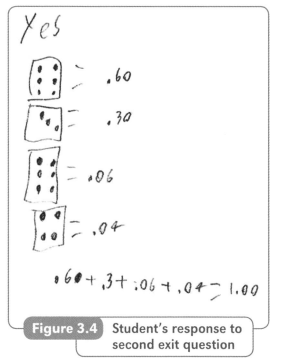

Figure 3.4 Student's response to second exit question

One student's response to the second exit question, shown in Figure 3.4, shows a range of concrete and abstract recordings. The student drew the die and recorded the decimal value of the rolls in the game. He also included an equation to show that the sum of the values was equal to one. Though the teacher understood the student's recordings with the die and the values he'd chosen for each roll, she noted that an equal sign should be used only with two quantities that have the same value. She wondered if she sometimes used this quick method of note taking as well, when she really meant "stands for" or "represents," perhaps unthinkingly supporting this misuse.

Extension

As a follow-up, students could investigate the following activity at a learning station, through an independent activity, or on an interactive bulletin board.

Number of Rolls to Win	Is it possible? Yes or No	Write a Winning Equation
1		
2		
3		
4		
5		
6		
7		
8		

Can You Make This Number?

Why This Game or Puzzle?

This game provides a motivating environment in which students can attend to ideas related to our number system. In this game, students must use the numbers they roll on dice as digits to try to form numbers that meet a set of given descriptions. The descriptions, for example, *Greater than 32 thousands*, include a variety of criteria involving numbers written in expanded form, stated comparisons, and identification of digits in a particular place value. Frequent opportunities to revisit such ideas are essential. "An underdeveloped understanding of place value can have far-reaching consequences" (Cooper and Tomayko 2011, 560). The quick pace of the game holds students' attention, and they gain an intuitive sense of which descriptions are more challenging to meet than others. Such intuition is applied to understanding, for example, whether they will be more or less likely to be able to form a number greater than 30,000 than form a number less than 12,000.

You can create your own descriptions for the game, depending on the ideas that you wish to emphasize, the size of the numbers you want students to consider, and whether you want the focus to be on whole numbers or decimals. Two sets of descriptions are provided on page A-16, along with room for students to record their responses. The rules of the game are relatively easy to understand, so once you've introduced it, students should be able to play it at a station with limited teacher direction.

Math Focus

› Recognizing place-value names
› Matching expanded form with the standard numeral form
› Rounding numbers

Materials Needed

› 5 dice per group of four students
› 1 *Can You Make This Number?* Game Board A or B per team (page A-16, top or bottom half)
› Optional: 1 *Can You Make This Number?* Directions per group (page A-17)

Can You Make This Number? **Game Board**

Name(s): _____ Date: _____

Game A

Descriptions	Roll	Number
a. Greater than 32 thousands	_____	__ __, __ __ __
b. 2 in the hundreds place	_____	__ __, __ __ __
c. Rounds to 31,000 when rounded to the nearest thousand	_____	__ __, __ __ __
d. Less than 20,000 + 400 + 3	_____	__ __, __ __ __
e. 1 in the hundreds place and 4 in the thousands place	_____	__ __, __ __ __
f. Between 43 thousands and 51 thousands	_____	__ __, __ __ __

Game B

Descriptions	Roll	Number
a. Less than 24	_____	_____
b. 3 in the hundredths place and 6 in the thousandths place	_____	_____
c. Greater than 45.214	_____	_____
d. Less than 25 + 0.3 + 0.56	_____	_____
e. 1 in the thousandths place and 3 in the tenths place	_____	_____
f. Rounds to 52.4 when rounded to the nearest tenth	_____	_____

Directions

Goal: Roll dice and use the numbers rolled as digits to try to form numbers to meet the given descriptions.

› One pair of students alternates turns with another pair of students.

› On its first turn, Team 1 rolls five dice and talks about how to use each of the numbers rolled as digits to form a number that can fit the first description on the game board.

› If the team can make a number to fit the description, it records the number and gives the dice to Team 2. On its next turn, Team 1 will try to make a number to fit the next description.

› If the team cannot make a number to fit the description, its turn ends and the team gives the dice to Team 2. Team 1 must roll and try again to meet the first description on its next turn.

› The teams continue to alternate turns, trying to make the numbers described in the order they appear on the game board.

› The first team to make all six numbers wins the game.

How It Looks in the Classroom

One fifth-grade teacher introduces this game briefly to the whole class by demonstrating a turn. She explains that the game is played by rolling five dice and then using the numbers rolled to make a number to fit a description. She displays the description *Less than 25,000.* She calls up two students and explains, "Your task is to roll these dice and try to make a number that will meet this description. Please record what you roll on the whiteboard and talk aloud so that we will know what you are thinking."

One student rolls and reports the outcomes as the other student records the numbers on the board. They have rolled 5, 3, 4, 3, 1. Paul says, "I don't think we can make it. We don't have a 2." He pauses and then asks, "Wait, can it be any number less than 25,000?"

His partner, Rosita, says, "Look, we can start with the 1 and then write the other digits any way we want." Once Paul agrees, they decide to write *13,543.*

The teacher asks the class if it is true that they could write any number they wanted as long as the 1 was in the ten thousands place. Nathan explains, "Yes, because all numbers in the ten thousands are less than all numbers in the twenty thousands." The teacher is pleased with the use of base ten language. She explains the rest of the rules, reminding students that they have to make a number, even if it takes several turns, before they can go on to the next description.

She has made two versions of the game board, to differentiate learning, and distributes the game boards accordingly.

Tips from the Classroom

〉 It may be best for some students who are unsure of themselves in new situations to start with a less challenging version of the game for the first round. Then once they have warmed up, they can move to a more difficult set of descriptions.

〉 Rolling the dice on a carpet square will silence the rolls.

〉 Some students may wish to arrange the dice on a place-value chart to help organize their thinking.

What to Look For

〉 What base ten terms do students use or not use?

〉 Do students recognize key numbers that they must roll to make the number described?

〉 Are students clear about the numbers that round to a given number?

〉 How do students think about descriptions with more than one criterion?

Variations

〉 As mentioned earlier, the specific descriptions can be changed to meet a variety of levels of learning. The number of dice rolled can also change.

❯ You could also change the rules to allow students to use the numbers rolled to meet any one of the descriptions, instead of requiring that they meet the descriptions in order. This change tends to create a more competitive game, as the initial turns of the game go quickly.

Exit Card Choices

❯ The description is *Greater than 53,413* (or *53.413*). You roll 2, 5, 4, 1, and 3. List the numbers you could make to fit this description.

❯ Which of the descriptions do you think is usually the most difficult to meet? Why?

Extension

Provide the following writing prompt for students to respond to individually or in pairs: *What five numbers could you roll to be able to meet all of the descriptions? Explain.*

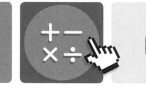

Online Games and Apps

Online games focus on a variety of skills related to base ten numeration; for example, there are many games that require players to identify the place value of a particular digit or to translate a number from one form to another before a bubble bursts or the time runs out. While often engaging for students because of the games' themes or the competition, many of these games do not utilize the power of the computer to assist students in learning more deeply about our base ten numeration system.

In contrast, games that provide students visual models of number relationships can offer learners access to conceptual understanding. Choices of difficulty levels also allow for differentiation. Following are some good examples:

• Look for number line games in which students are given a number, such as 832, to locate on a number line. Players begin by choosing a range of numbers that the target number is within. Each time they choose a range of numbers, they see the number line zoomed in to a smaller range of numbers, getting them closer and closer to the correct place on the line. The player who uses the least number of moves to get to the correct location is the winner. Such online games often offer teachers and players the ability to make number lines of different lengths or to specify different ranges of numbers, including determining whether players will work with only whole numbers or will work with decimals as well. One example of such a (free) game can be found on an Oxford University Press website at http://www.oup.com.au/__data/assets/file/0019/154045/Numberline.swf. The student is given a number and must choose what range of numbers the given number is within, choosing from 1–100; 100–1,000; 1,000–10,000; and so forth. If the student chooses 10,000–100,000 for the number 79,219, the number line begins moving across the screen until the student chooses the range 70,000–80,000. Eventually the range is narrowed to the point where the student can identify the target number.

- Motion Math Zoom (http://motionmathgames.com/motion-math-zoom/) is an app that requires students to find the correct place for a number on a stretchable number line as it is moving. The numbers are represented as animals of various sizes, such as dinosaurs for large numbers and amoebas for small numbers. This app also allows students to practice number placement with decimals and negative numbers.

- Another app, Tick Bait's Universe (http://www.youuapps.com/products/tick-baits-universe/), integrates math and science learning, relating greater and smaller numbers to zoomed in (or out) views of the world. As students pinch the screen, the universe is made larger or smaller by a power of ten, allowing views as small as bacteria and as large as the outer planets as related to 0.0001 m and 1,000,000 m, respectively. Students may explore the universe or engage in the Scavenger Hunt game, looking for objects shown from different views, allowing for players to visualize small and large numbers within a real-world context.

When playing online games, students should still be expected to provide evidence of their learning. For example, if playing a number line game, students may be asked to record their moves in order to practice writing numbers and to allow the teacher to assess students' learning once the activity is complete. You may also ask students to answer questions about what they learned while completing a game, such as *To what number of meters do you think that you would need to zoom to view the planets?* or *What is the least number of moves that you needed to find your target number?*

4

Addition and Subtraction

What's the Math?

Addition and subtraction with whole numbers is the computation focus for grades K–2. In grades 3–5, students expand their thinking to the development of accurate algorithms that can be applied efficiently, regardless of the particular whole numbers involved. In fifth grade, students extend such thinking to the addition and subtraction of decimals. Students also need to further develop their ability to estimate sums and differences and recognize the relationships among the numbers in an addition or subtraction equation.

Games and puzzles serve as excellent vehicles for maintaining and expanding these concepts and skills. As conceptual development and fluency must be intertwined goals of students' learning, the games and puzzles you choose for instructional purposes should involve deductive reasoning, conjecturing, and proving or disproving. Hillen and Watanabe (2013) identify such thinking as the essence of mathematics. Though we acknowledge that some students in grades 3–5 may continue to need practice with gaining fluency with addition and subtraction facts, that goal is not considered in this chapter. However, such fluency may improve through tasks involving greater numbers or decimal numbers.

While important for all students, continued attention to addition and subtraction for students with learning difficulties is essential. These students may remain inaccurate when computing; lack an understanding of place-value relationships; or treat each column in a vertically arranged computation example as a separate problem, without understanding relationships between the columns (Mundia 2012). Further, their lack of understanding may cause them to hold on to inefficient strategies such as counting on or back by ones. These games and puzzles provide such students with engaging tasks as well as access to how other students think about these operations.

What's Your Problem?

Why This Game or Puzzle?

Developing students' understanding of addition and subtraction, rather than having them merely apply rote procedures, is a complex goal. To achieve it, we must offer our students many opportunities to discuss their strategies and to recognize the relationships among the numbers in any addition or subtraction equation. As with any goal, it should serve as our focus as we steer students' talk about mathematics (Kazemi and Hintz 2014). Providing tasks that highlight such relationships gives students something to discuss.

In this game, one team creates an addition problem and the other team tries to identify each digit in the problem, within fifteen guesses. The game stimulates such thinking as *If the sum in the tens column is seven, and one of the addends' digits in that column is nine, what do we know?* and *If we have already learned that there is not an eight in that column, what do I know?* The limited number of guesses can motivate teams to consider ideas like these so that they use their guesses as wisely as possible.

What's Your Problem? Game Board

Name(s): _____   Date: _____

The Knower Board

Line 1   _____ _____ _____
Line 2   +   _____ _____ _____
              _____
Line 3   _____ _____ _____

Name(s): _____   Date: _____

The Guesser Board

Line 1   _____ _____ _____
Line 2   +   _____ _____ _____
              _____
Line 3   _____ _____ _____

Math Focus

› Understanding relationships between addition and subtraction
› Adding and subtracting

Materials Needed

› 1 *What's Your Problem?* Game Board per team (page A-18)
› Optional: 1 *What's Your Problem?* Directions per group (page A-19)

Directions

Goal: Identify all the digits in a mystery problem within fifteen guesses.

› Take turns being the "knower" and the "guesser" teams. Use different parts of your game board as you do so.

› The knower team creates and solves an addition problem involving two three-digit numbers on the knower part of the board, taking care to compute accurately.

› The guesser team asks questions in the following format: *Are there any _____ s in the _____ column?* For example, the guesser might ask, "Are there any 3s in the ones column?"

› If the guesser team is correct about the number *and* the column, the knower team answers by telling which line in that column the number is on. If there is more than one such number in the column, the knower team identifies all of them. The guesser team records this information on its game board.

› If the guesser team is incorrect about *either* the number or the column, the knower team says, "No, there is no 3 in the ones column." To keep track of the number of guesses used, a guesser team player marks an *x* on one of the fifteen lines below the computation example for each question his or her team asks.

› A guesser player may ask, "Is there a 4 in the ones column and a 2 in the tens column?" If both parts of the guess are not correct, the answer will be "No."

› If the guesser team does not figure out the computation problem within fifteen questions, the knower team reveals the answer and the teams exchange roles.

How It Looks in the Classroom

One fourth-grade teacher begins by asking the students, "How many of you have watched or played the game Wheel of Fortune?" All but a couple of students raise their hands, and he asks a few of them to describe the game to those who are not familiar with it. The students explain the basic rules. Then the teacher asks the students to talk with their neighbors about strategies for guessing letters. After a brief time he asks, "How do you decide which letters to guess?"

Ari says, "It's best to always start with vowels."

Other students agree and then the teacher asks, "How does knowing one letter help you to decide another?"

Trina says, "Well, some letters just go together, and others wouldn't make sense."

Josephina adds, "Yes, like if the first letter is *z*, then the next letter has to be a vowel, but other letters, like *c*, could have a vowel or maybe another consonant."

The teacher then introduces *What's Your Problem?* by writing the diagram in Figure 4.1 on the board. He tells them that the game is somewhat like the Wheel of Fortune game, but in this game their job is to find all of the numbers in a math problem. He says, "You have fifteen guesses and you need to think about numbers that go together and make sense." He then explains that to guess, they must ask questions in a certain format: *Is there a (say the number) in the (say a place-value column)?*

Line 1 _____ _____ _____

Line 2   +   _____ _____ _____

Line 3 _____ _____ _____ _____

Figure 4.1 *What's Your Problem?* example

Benita begins the practice game by asking, "Is there a 6 in the tens column?"

The teacher announces, "No, there is not a 6 in the tens column." Then he makes an *x* on the board to show that they have used one guess.

Denzel asks, "Is there a 4 in the hundreds column?"

The teacher says, "Yes," and writes a 4 on the first and third lines.

Conrad says, "So there has to be a 0 in line 2, right?"

Nani responds, "Wait, there can't be a 0 because there is an extra digit in the sum."

The teacher encourages everyone to turn and talk with a neighbor. After this chance to reflect with peers, the class makes a guess using the appropriate format to confirm that there must be regrouping from the tens column, the number in line 2 of the hundreds column must be 9, and the first digit in line 3 must be 1. The teacher writes in these correct numbers, as shown in Figure 4.2.

Line 1 ____4____ _____ _____

Line 2   +   ____9____ _____ _____

Line 3 ___1___ ___4___ _____ _____

Figure 4.2 Status of the game after four guesses

Tips from the Classroom

❯ Some guessers may be able to better keep track of their guesses if they make a place-value diagram and list their guesses for each column.

❯ Students tend to forget about regrouping. One team who began with asking about 9s in the tens column learned that there were three of them. Rather than reacting with excitement about the number of digits this one question had provided them, players were certain the information was incorrect, as nine plus nine could not be nine. In situations like this, encourage students to keep guessing so that more of the computation will be revealed.

What to Look For

❯ Do students consider regrouping before making a guess?

❯ Do students recognize that the digit in the thousands place must be 1?

❯ How do students keep track of the information they gain from their incorrect guesses?

Variations

❯ Have students create problems with two- or four-digit numbers rather than three-digit numbers.

❯ Keep the number of digits in each line the same and play the game with subtraction problems. Then play with both operations, but have the knower team refrain from telling the guesser team whether it is an addition or subtraction problem. The guesser team has to figure that out over the course of the game.

❯ You could add the rule *No repeated digits may be placed in different columns of the problem* to the game, eliminating several choices for the guesser team.

Exit Card Choices

❯ Your game board looks like this:

```
┌─────────────────────────────────────────────────────┐
│                                                       │
│   The Guesser Board                                   │
│                                                       │
│   Line 1        _____    ___7___    _____     │
│                                                       │
│   Line 2   +    _____    ___3___    _____     │
│                                                       │
│                ──────────────────────────────────    │
│                                                       │
│   Line 3        _____    _____    _____   │
│                                                       │
└─────────────────────────────────────────────────────┘
```

❯ What numbers could you guess for line 3 of the tens column, and why?

❯ What might be a good first guess to make? Why?

❯ If you were on the knower team what strategies could you use to create a challenging problem? An easier problem?

Extension

Have students create *What's the Problem?* puzzles, in which all of the missing digits can be determined. Each letter in an individual problem always represents the same missing digit. For example:

```
    7 A B
  + B 3 9
  ———————
  1 C 8 5
```

Tic-Tic-Tac-Toe

Why This Game or Puzzle?

Estimation skills are essential; we likely use them every day. We estimate when exact answers are not required and to check the reasonableness of computation completed with paper and pencil or an electronic device. For instance, in a grocery store, we may estimate to see if we have enough money for what we are purchasing and then estimate again to make sure the total the cashier tells us makes sense. According to Lan and colleagues, "Computational estimation is a complex skill involving many of the same subtleties and complexities as problem solving" (2010, 1). Unfortunately, most of the opportunities students have to practice their computational skills are focused on finding exact answers.

In this game, students are given two sets of numbers. They choose a number from each set, find their total, and write an *X* (or an *O*) on the sum on the game board. The goal is to write an *X* (or an *O*) on four adjacent sums in a row, column, or diagonal. This aspect of the game encourages students to estimate sums when choosing addends, make conjectures, plan ahead, and decide when they want to block an opponent's move. When we field-tested it, students told us to make the game board look more like a tic-tac-toe game, so we eliminated the outside borders. Two versions of the game are included; version 2 uses greater numbers.

Math Focus

› Adding multidigit numbers
› Estimating sums

Tic-Tic-Tac-Toe Game 1 Game Board

	Sign A			Sign B	
361		425	47		175
	345			516	
256		119	269		56

408	294	941	525	401
520	694	312	877	303
772	175	536	392	388
417	472	614	431	635

Materials Needed

› 1 *Tic-Tic-Tac-Toe* Game 1 or Game 2 Game Board per group of players (page A-20 or A-21)
› Optional: 1 *Tic-Tic-Tac-Toe* Directions per group (page A-22)

Directions

Goal: Choose addends in order to mark off four sums in a row, column, or diagonal on the game board.

› Decide which team will be *X* and which will be *O*. The first team picks a number from Sign A and one from Sign B. Both teams compute the sum. (Teams get to pick only once, even if they discover that they don't get a sum they want.)
› Once both teams have confirmed the sum, the first team finds it on the game board and writes the team's mark (*X* or *O*) in that space.
› If the team gets a sum that is already marked with an *X* or an *O*, it loses its turn.
› Teams alternate turns.
› The first team to write its mark in four touching sums in a row, column, or diagonal is the winner. These *X*'s are in the same row and touch:

These *X*'s are in the same row but do not all touch:

X	X	X		X

How It Looks in the Classroom

One third-grade teacher displays the expression 354 + 481 as well as the three numbers 732, 845, and 645. She says, "I am going to count slowly to three. By the time I get to three, I want you to have chosen which of these three numbers is the sum." As she counts, she notes the expressions on the students' faces. She notices that some of them look nervous, while others appear quite confident.

Nick reports that he didn't have enough time to add the numbers. Shauna tells how she eliminated 732 right away, by adding the ones digits. Diego says, "It has to be 845, because there are seven hundreds and there is regrouping." Many students agree and a few of them share that they were confused because they were sure the number had to begin with a 7.

The teacher displays *Tic-Tic-Tac-Toe Directions* (page A-22), tells the students that predicting sums is a focus of this game, reviews the rules of play, and makes sure students understand what it means for sums to be "touching." Players then form teams, get copies of the game board, and begin playing.

Tips from the Classroom

❯ Some students are likely to begin by choosing numbers randomly. It's best not to intervene too quickly. After a couple of turns, players often use estimation to make better choices for addends.

❯ It can be helpful to ask players to think aloud as they choose their addends, as their thinking gives other students access to a variety of strategies.

❯ You may wish to allow some opponents to use calculators to check sums after they have estimated.

❯ A couple of students may decide to find all of the sums before playing the game. Help them understand that the purpose of the game is to choose addends within a short time span, encouraging estimation instead of computing exact answers before making choices.

❯ You may need to remind players that both teams are expected to find each sum, as a way to check for accuracy. Sometimes opponents become so focused on their next move that they forget this aspect of the game.

What to Look For

❯ Do students choose addends randomly or do they use strategies for making choices?

❯ What mathematical language do students use to describe their thinking?

❯ What strategies do students use to help them get four touching numbers in a row, column, or diagonal?

❯ Do students remember to block opponents when necessary?

❯ What do teams do if they disagree about a sum?

Variations

❱ In our field-testing, one group of students suggested the game rule: if a team calculates a sum incorrectly, it loses its turn. This rule motivated opposing teams to check calculations.

❱ By changing the numbers on the signs and the game board, you can vary this game, having students find differences, products, or quotients. You could also include decimals.

Exit Card Choices

❱ What strategies did you use to choose your addends on your turns?

❱ When did you think it was important to block an opponent rather than find a sum that touched the sums you already had?

❱ What did you do if you and your opponents disagreed on a sum?

Figure 4.3 shows one team's response to the first exit card. The students were able to communicate how their strategy for choosing addends developed as they played the game.

First we chose by looking at the ones place. When we didn't get the sum we wanted, we learned that sometimes there was more than one choice that gave the same total in the ones colum. Then we used the hundreds digits. That didn't always work. Sometimes there was regrouping from the tens. So now we try to look at the right and left digits as quickly as we can.

Figure 4.3 Response to the first exit card

Extension

Have students create, exchange, and play their own versions of the game. They choose the five numbers for each sign, compute the related twenty-five possible sums, replace any combinations that don't provide unique sums, and then randomly write the sums on the game board.

Game adapted from *Four in a Row* in *Zeroing in on Number and Operations: Key Ideas and Common Misconceptions, Grades 3–4*, by Linda Dacey and Anne Collins (Portland, ME: Stenhouse, 2010).

Logical Numbers

Why This Game or Puzzle?

In real life, information may be stated implicitly, rather than explicitly, requiring the ability to use deductive reasoning. Also, information may be redundant or need to be combined to be most useful. Too often, we give students mathematical tasks that provide all of the information explicitly, without extra data, and already in the order that is needed for use.

Logical Numbers puzzles require solvers to interpret and combine clues to identify the solution. They also provide the opportunity for students to learn, if they do not already know, how a table can be used to organize information. Visual organization of data can support students' conceptual understanding (Farbermann and Musina 2004), and it is important to expose students to a variety of visual formats.

Two levels of the puzzle are provided, offering differences in both the size of the numbers and the complexity of the logical thinking. Some students working with addition and subtraction with greater numbers may still benefit from beginning with the first puzzle.

Logical Numbers **Puzzle A**

Name(s): _____   Date: _____

Five friends are running in a race to raise money to build a new playground. Their race bib numbers are 337, 135, 142, 632, and 545.
Use the clues to find the number each racer is wearing.
  1. The sum of Mica's and Cooper's race numbers is an even number.
  2. If you add Isabella's race number to itself, the sum is 674.
  3. If you subtract Jordana's race number from Mica's race number, the difference is greater than 200.
  4. The difference between Jordana's race number and Isabella's race number is less than 200.
  5. Riley's race number is equal to 906 − 342 + 68.

	Names				
Race Numbers					

The race number for Mica is _____.

The race number Cooper for is _____.

The race number for Isabella is _____.

The race number for Riley is _____.

The race number for Jordana is _____.

Math Focus

› Finding sums and differences
› Estimating sums and differences

Materials Needed

› 1 *Logical Numbers* Puzzle A or B per student or pair (page A-23 or A-24)
› Optional: 1 *Logical Numbers* Directions per student or pair (page A-25)
› Optional: 1 calculator per student

Directions

Goal: Use the clues to match the right pieces of information with each other (for example, race bib numbers with racers and codes with types of locks).

⟩ Work alone or with a partner.

⟩ Read the clues.

⟩ Use the table to organize what you know from each clue.

⟩ Make notes so that you can recall your thinking. Include computation and clue numbers in your notes.

⟩ You do not need to use the clues in order.

⟩ Check your solution with each clue.

How It Looks in the Classroom

A teacher introduces a *Logical Numbers* puzzle by asking, "How many of you have read stories about Encyclopedia Brown, Harriet the Spy, or Jigsaw Jones? What can you tell me about them and what they did?" As the students share ideas, the teacher records key words, such as *mysteries*, *solves*, *uses clues*, and *detective*. She then displays the mini-puzzle shown in Figure 4.4 and explains that they are going to be math detectives. Her goal is to model ways of gleaning information from clues and use of the table to record that information.

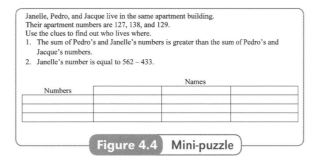

Janelle, Pedro, and Jacque live in the same apartment building.
Their apartment numbers are 127, 138, and 129.
Use the clues to find out who lives where.
1. The sum of Pedro's and Janelle's numbers is greater than the sum of Pedro's and Jacque's numbers.
2. Janelle's number is equal to 562 − 433.

Figure 4.4 Mini-puzzle

She points to the chart and asks what the students think should be written in the first row and first column. Following their suggestions, she adds the names and numbers to the chart. Then she tells them to read the first clue and turn and talk to a neighbor about what it tells them. Krista summarizes the students' thinking by saying, "This was hard at first, but we decided that Janelle's number has to be bigger than Jacque's."

Once Krista's thinking is discussed further, the teacher asks, "So what does that tell us about Jacque's number?"

Ivan becomes excited and declares, "One hundred thirty-eight is the greatest number. So Jacque can't be 138." Once others agree, the teacher models how to use the chart by marking an *X* in the cell that connects Jacque to 138.

"What about the next clue?" the teacher asks. Students complete the subtraction and readily identify Janelle's number as 129. The teacher draws a star in the appropriate cell to indicate this information and then asks, "What other numbers can we cross out, knowing that Janelle is 129? Can anyone else be 129? Can Janelle live anywhere else?" The completed chart is shown in Figure 4.5.

Numbers	Names		
	Janelle	Pedro	Jacque
127	X	X	★
138	X	★	X
129	★	X	X

Figure 4.5 Completed table

Before the teacher releases the students to investigate another *Logical Numbers* puzzle individually or in pairs, the class explores the question *What would happen if we read the second clue first?*

Tips from the Classroom

❭ Some students may find it easier to organize information in a list. For example, they could write all possible race numbers under each racer's name and then cross out numbers they eliminate and circle numbers they identify.

❭ Making calculators available may allow some students to give greater attention to the deductive reasoning required.

❭ In our field testing, some teachers were concerned that the puzzles might be too challenging but were surprised by what students could understand when they worked together.

❭ You can provide more challenge by giving students the clues without a copy of the chart, requiring students to determine their own way to keep track of their possible solutions.

❭ If necessary, you may wish to highlight clues 2 and 5 for Puzzles A and B for some students and suggest they consider these clues first.

❭ Be sure students use pencils, or laminate the charts and have students use dry-erase markers, so that solvers can easily erase their work and begin again when necessary. Alternatively, students could have multiple copies of the chart so that they can refer back to previous work if they choose to.

What to Look For

❭ Are there any vocabulary words students find challenging or confusing?

❭ Do students use the clues in an efficient order?

❭ How do students record information that indicates relationships among the codes?

❭ Which students use estimation to narrow the choices?

❭ Do students check their solutions?

❭ How successful are students in describing their solution paths to others?

Variations

❯ Create puzzles with decimal numbers in contexts such as money, miles driven, or race times.

❯ Have students complete the puzzle in a group of five, giving each student only one of the clues. (See *Name That Number,* page 121.)

Exit Card Choices

❯ What different computation example could you write for the fifth clue? It must have two subtraction signs and one addition sign.

❯ Which clue did you think/talk the most about? Why?

❯ What clue was most useful to you? Why?

Extension

❯ Have students participate in a debate as to whether solvers should first read all the clues carefully, in order, or skim the clues to find the best clue with which to start.

Subtracto Draw

Why This Game or Puzzle?

Predicting when it will be necessary to regroup and understanding the impact of regrouping on related numbers is an important aspect of understanding traditional algorithms for addition and subtraction, mental computation, and estimation. These concepts help us recognize that the answer to an expression such as 100 − 46 will be in the fifties before we begin to determine the exact difference. Similarly, by examining whether or not regrouping is needed, we can recognize that 452 + 592 will result in a four-digit sum. It is important to recognize that computational thinking extends well beyond finding exact answers. Huinker, Freckman, and Steinmeyer (2003) suggest that meaningful computation occurs when number relationships, understanding of operations, and children's ways of thinking are combined.

Target games provide opportunities for students to think about relationships among numbers, to estimate, and then to compute exact answers. There is also a bit of tension and luck involved, which tends to add interest for most students. In this target game, there are allotted spaces to write digits to form two numbers in a subtraction expression, along with a target number for the difference. Students turn over cards one at a time and write each digit in an empty space. When all spaces are filled, players compute the subtraction problems they have created and check the resulting differences against the target number. The player whose difference is closest to the target number wins.

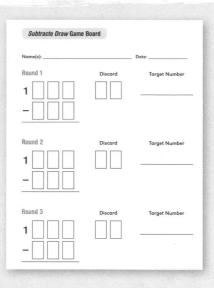

Math Focus

› Computing differences
› Estimating differences

Materials Needed

› 1 *Subtracto Draw* Game Board per team (page A-26)
› 1 deck of *Subtracto Draw* Cards per group of players (page A-27)
› Optional: 1 *Subtracto Draw* Directions per group (page A-28)

Directions

Goal: Place digits to create a subtraction example with a difference closest to the target number.

› Shuffle the cards and place them facedown. Choose one student to be the card turner. That student turns over the top three cards to form a three-digit number. Each team writes this number on its recording sheet as the target number for the round.

› Place those three cards back in the deck and shuffle the cards again.

› The card turner turns over the top card of the deck, and each team decides privately where to write the number in the subtraction example for round 1 or to write it in the discard area. Once the team has written a number, it can't move the number to another space.

› Turn over the next card and decide where to place that digit.

› After eight cards have been turned over and recorded, teams subtract to find their differences.

› Teams exchange papers to check each other's subtraction.

› Teams then return papers and determine together which team found a difference closest to the target number. That team gets a point for that round.

› After three rounds, the team with more points wins.

How It Looks in the Classroom

One fourth-grade teacher introduces the game by reminding the students of their school's goal of making 1,000 paper cranes. He says, "Talk with a partner about what it means to set a target, and identify some targets or goals you have tried to meet." There is an immediate buzz in the room as partners begin their discussions. He hears some students talk about physical targets such as how fast they swim or how long they run. Other students refer to goals set at home such as making their beds every day or getting along better with siblings.

Next the teacher asks, "What do you do when you are trying to meet a target?"

Donovan reports that he keeps it in mind and that he has a card on his mirror that reads, *You can do it!*

Maya says, "It's good to check in about it. I want to be sure my mom notices that I am being nice to my younger sister."

The teacher summarizes the discussion by saying, "It's great that you keep your targets in mind and check in on how you are doing as you try to meet them. We're going to apply that kind of thinking to a math game." He then draws the subtraction example as shown in Figure 4.6 on the board and tells the students to draw the same figure in their journals. He explains that he has shuffled cards labeled 0–9 and that they will use the cards to identify numbers to write in the boxes. He turns over the first three cards to form the target number, which he and the students record. Then he returns these cards, reshuffles, and turns over the next card and explains that they may choose to place it in one of the spaces in the subtraction example or in a discard space. He then announces, "Think carefully about your choice, as you can't change it later." The class completes the game, after which there is much interest in playing it again. Teams are formed and the students play in small groups.

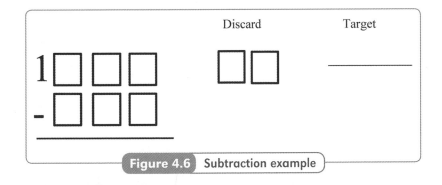

Figure 4.6 Subtraction example

Tips from the Classroom

❱ Most students need to play a few rounds before they begin to think strategically. Provide the opportunity for such play, without leading their thinking.

❱ After a round of play, encourage students with different placements of numbers to share their thinking.

 〉 We found that the most frequently discarded number was 0. A few students told us it was because 0 wasn't worth anything. Some others told us it was because 0's were hard to use in subtraction. Note the numbers your students discard to see if there is a pattern that should be addressed.

 〉 You may wish to have your students use a pen while playing this game so that they are less tempted to change their answers.

What to Look For

 〉 Do some students appear to write a number randomly? Do others seem to take quite a while to decide where to write a digit?

 〉 Do students recognize that 0 cannot be the first digit in a three-digit number?

 〉 Is there a pattern to the three-digit numbers that students form? Is there a pattern among the numbers they discard?

 〉 What evidence is there that students plan ahead when they discuss where to write a number?

 〉 Do students think about how regrouping will impact the difference they will get?

Variations

 〉 Have students use addition to try to get close to the target.

 〉 Add extra digits to the numbers in the problem by adding a box to each number in the subtraction example and allowing only one discard.

 〉 Include decimal points in the template as appropriate for your students.

 〉 Remove the 1s in the thousands places on the recording sheet before copying so students won't have to regroup thousands and hundreds. We found that when students who used such a recording sheet created an example with a negative difference, they decided that their example did not work.

Exit Card Choices

 〉 What reasons did you have for placing numbers in the discard spaces?

 〉 What did you learn about subtraction by playing this game?

 〉 How does thinking about regrouping help you place the digits?

The student work in Figure 4.7, written in response to the last exit card question, shows how a team began to realize the importance of thinking about regrouping when it decided where to place its numbers.

Sometime we discarded a number because
we didn't think. It would work.
Then when we placed other numbers in
the column to the right and it turned out
regrouping would be necessary.
If we had thought about regrouping our
discarded number would have been perfect.
You don't know what is going to happen,
So you have to remember about
regrouping.

Figure 4.7 Response to the last exit card

Extension

Have students respond to the following task individually or in pairs: *The numbers drawn are 3, 4, 5, 6, 7, and 8. List the different arrangements you can find that have a difference between 500 and 550.*

Adapted from *Subtracto Draw* in *Zeroing in on Number and Operations: Key Ideas and Common Misconceptions, Grades 3–4,* by Linda Dacey and Anne Collins (Portland, ME: Stenhouse, 2010).

Double Decimal Dilemma

Why This Game or Puzzle?

Mental arithmetic is an important skill. It supports estimation, and in some situations, it is the only computational technique that makes sense. Researchers agree that mental arithmetic is important but have not yet agreed as to whether mental arithmetic strategies should be developed by students on their own or be explicitly taught (Varol and Farran 2007). Regardless of where your views are on that continuum, students need opportunities to develop mental arithmetic strategies and skills.

This game is adapted from a popular one often called Pig or Double Out, in which students roll dice to try to attain a certain score first. When they roll the dice, they find the sum mentally and keep rolling and adding until they decide their turn is over or they roll doubles. If they roll doubles, the score from that turn is 0, though they can keep scores from previous turns. In this version, the focus is on adding decimal numbers.

The numbers on the dice represent tenths (i.e., a 1 on a die represents 0.1). As written, it is most appropriate for students working at the fifth-grade level; variations for other grade levels are suggested.

Math Focus

› Adding tenths mentally and with paper and pencil

Materials Needed

› 2 dice per group of players
› 1 calculator per group
› 1 *Double Decimal Dilemma* Recording Sheet per team (page A-29)
› Optional: 1 *Double Decimal Dilemma* Directions per group (page A-30)

Double Decimal Dilemma **Recording Sheet**

Name(s): _____   Date: _____

	Points for Round	Total Points
Round 1		
Round 2		
Round 3		
Round 4		
Round 5		
Round 6		
Round 7		
Round 8		

Directions

Goal: Roll dice and use mental computation to reach a total score of 15 (or more).

› You will be rolling dice and finding the sum of the numbers you roll. The numbers on the dice represent tenths. For example, if you roll a 1, that represents 0.1.

› Take turns. On each turn you should roll the two dice and find their sum. Continue rolling and adding each new sum, using mental arithmetic, to your previous total.

› End your turn by handing the dice to your opponent when

  › you decide it's best to end your turn to secure your score;

  › your opponent correctly challenges your mental arithmetic, which requires you to end your turn and go back to the mental sum you acquired before your error (challenges can be checked with calculators); or

  › you roll doubles, which means you lose your turn and your score for this round returns to 0.

› After each turn, record the total for this round, which remains part of your total score no matter what happens on your future turns, and find and record your running total.

› The game ends when one team reaches a score of 15 or more.

How It Looks in the Classroom

One fifth-grade teacher decides to demonstrate a turn. She tells the students that the game involves rolling dice, which represent tenths, and finding the sum. She gives two dice to a student, who rolls a 5 and a 6. She says, "Use mental arithmetic to find the sum of five-tenths and six-tenths."

"That's simple: eleven-tenths," Jordan responds.

The teacher tells students to talk to their neighbors about whether they think Jordan's answer is correct. There is not clear agreement. The class finally decides that the answer is eleven-tenths, but that it is also one and one-tenth. The teacher clarifies that for this game, they will always trade tenths for ones when it is possible to do so.

Then the teacher gives the dice to another student to roll, and this time, the numbers on the dice represent three-tenths and four-tenths. The teacher says, "So now you have to find the sum of these two numbers and add it to your last sum. What do you get?" Once this arithmetic is completed, the teacher says, "So you can keep rolling and adding as many times as you want, and the first player to reach a total greater than or equal to fifteen wins. Does that sound like an interesting game?"

"Wait," Dylan says. "If you can roll as many times as you want, how does your opponent ever get a turn?"

"Ah," says the teacher, "that's the interesting part." She then explains the ways turns may end, reviews all the game rules, and asks a student from each table to gather dice and recording sheets for the players at the table.

Tips from the Classroom

❯ To emphasize the use of decimals, you may wish to put small stickers on each side of the dice, labeled with the decimal numbers 0.1, 0.2, 0.3, and so on.

❯ Students may struggle in the beginning, particularly if they have limited experience with using mental arithmetic to add decimals. You could allow them to use paper and pencil for a few rounds and then switch to mental arithmetic.

❯ Thinking about money may be helpful. During one turn we heard Abigail explain, "I have eight-tenths from my last roll, and six-tenths here. That's like eight dimes and six dimes, which is a dollar and four dimes, one dollar and forty cents, or one and four-tenths."

❯ Some students may experience difficulty remembering their previous sums within a round. Allow them to roll the dice, add by using mental arithmetic, and then record this subtotal. When they roll next, they should again add without paper and pencil, then cross out the previous subtotal and record the new one.

❯ Some students may come to realize that they can add as if the dice represented whole numbers and just convert to tenths when recording the sums. This is an important mathematical realization and mental arithmetic strategy, which students should make on their own. Once this thinking becomes routine for some students, have them consider a more challenging variation of the game.

What to Look For

❭ What strategies do students use to find sums?

❭ What do you notice about when students decide to end their turns? Do some students always roll three or fewer times? Do others usually roll until they get doubles?

Variations

❭ Some students suggested that if you roll double 6s, you should lose all the points collected so far, even in previous rounds. Students had strong positive and negative reactions to this suggestion. You could allow players to decide whether or not they want to include this rule or one like it.

❭ Third and fourth graders can play this game with whole numbers and a goal of 150.

❭ To provide more challenge, have students use three dice with the rule that if the sum for a roll is seven- or eight-tenths (or ones), which has the same probability of rolling doubles with two dice, you get 0 points for that turn. The goal number would be 22 (or 220).

❭ To simplify the game, use one die, with the goal of reaching 8 (or 80), and have the rule be that if you roll a 3, which has the same probability of rolling doubles with two dice, you get 0 points for that turn.

❭ Students can investigate this game in a solitaire format and see how many turns it takes to get to the goal number.

Exit Card Choices

❭ What strategies do you use to add mentally?

❭ How did you decide when to end your turn?

Extension

Some students may wish to explore the probability of rolling doubles by drawing conclusions from experimental data. Have each student roll the dice until doubles occur and record how many rolls it took. Each student should do this five times. Create a line plot to summarize the class data.

Adapted from *The Game of Pig* in *About Teaching Mathematics* by Marilyn Burns (Sausalito, CA: Math Solutions, 1997).

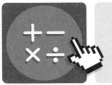

Online Games and Apps

Many technology-based addition and subtraction games focus primarily on the practice of basic facts. They often provide the player with an extrinsic reward for accurately completing a problem, such as the opportunity to shoot a target or "win" a prize. Online games and apps that require an account can often be adapted to a particular user's needs, differentiating by incorporating known facts with those still needing attention. These types of fact games help students master their facts and often provide an engaging environment in which to practice.

In contrast, technology-based games that require students to incorporate their practice of math facts in a real-world context or to use flexible thinking provide students with the opportunity to go beyond memorization. Following are some examples:

- Kakooma (free), found on Greg Tang's website (http://www.gregtangmath.com/), may be played online or through an app. Students may play individually or with others through a multiplayer option. The goal of the addition version of Kakooma is to find the number that is the sum of two others in a group of numbers. Because students must choose the correct sum from among four to nine numbers (depending on the level), flexible thinking must be employed as students consider a variety of choices. Oftentimes, the player ends up doing a great deal of mental math in order to find the correct answer. There are various ways to increase the difficulty level, by increasing the size of the puzzle, including more numbers to choose from, and providing a greater target sum. This game encourages efficiency by timing students' completion rates and focuses on accuracy by discouraging students from making incorrect guesses. Competition with other puzzlers can include solvers all over the world.

- The app Wuzzit Trouble (http://www.wuzzittrouble.com/) is a logic and problem-solving game in which students must find keys in order to free Wuzzits. Players are required to find combinations of numbers that will rotate gears in order to unlock the necessary keys. For example, a large gear, marked off in 5s, is shown with keys available at 15, 40, and 55 and a starting value of 0. The small attached gear will move in groups of 10. Students must figure out how to move the small gear in either a clockwise or counterclockwise direction so that all of the keys are collected. This task may take several moves and consideration of how to combine the numbers in order to collect all the keys in the least number of moves. Many levels of difficulty provide students with a game-based environment in which they can experiment with a variety of possibilities and solve problems for a purpose.

● Circle 99, a free puzzle available on the National Library of Virtual Manipulatives website (http://nlvm.usu.edu/en/nav/vlibrary.html; click on "Number & Operations," and then click on "Circle 99" in the list), presents five stationary numbers and nine that can be moved inside a ring of interlocking circles similar to Venn diagrams. Students must place the moveable numbers inside the interlocking circles so that the sum within each circle is ninety-nine. Students may choose to use the guess-and-check method for placing the numbers, relationships among numbers, and mental math strategies. In all cases, students are required to evaluate many one- and two-digit addition problems, practicing inference and number logic to find a correct solution.

Multiplication and Division

What's the Math?

Learning about multiplication and division is a major focus of the curriculum in grades 3 through 5. Usually the concepts are introduced in third grade, and emphasis is placed on the equal-groups meaning of the operations, the relationship between these operations, and the goal of achieving fluency with basic multiplication facts. In fourth grade, factors and multiples are explored, the operations are extended to greater numbers using strategies and properties, and remainders are introduced. By fifth grade, use of a standard algorithm for multiplication is often expected and computation is extended to hundredths. With such growth in expectations over these three years, students need many opportunities to deepen their conceptual understanding and practice their skills.

Most teachers know a variety of games, websites, and apps for practicing multiplication with single-digit numbers but tend to have fewer resources that require players or puzzlers to make mathematical decisions other than identify a product or quotient. Understanding patterns within and among multiples helps students develop fact strategies and eventually reach fluency. The combination of conceptual understanding, procedural fluency, and fact recall reinforces children's learning (National Mathematics Advisory Panel 2008).

Many teachers tell us that they wish they knew more games and puzzles for working with greater numbers and for division, with and without remainders. Students find division challenging for a variety of reasons, and remainders are particularly problematic. Traditional algorithms for multiplication and division are complex and rarely understood deeply by students (Fuson 2003). Activities that engage students in conversations about these operations and deepen their understanding of the relationships between them are essential, if students are to make sense of these multistep procedures.

 **Table Topper**

Why This Game or Puzzle?

When we first started writing this book, we asked several teachers, "What's the one game that you can't live without?" Using several different titles, they all described this classic game, and we agree that this game is special. We present it here with a new title, as we want to draw students' attention to the term *table*, to name the format used to summarize all of the basic facts included. Presenting the facts in this form reinforces the array model of multiplication, which, unlike a number line model, emphasizes the idea that multiplication is much more than repeated addition.

Unlike many opportunities to practice basic fact knowledge, this game includes strategic thinking. The goal of "topping" four products in a row, column, or diagonal encourages students to consider a variety of alternatives and contemplate such ideas as *Which product is surrounded by other products that have several factors? If I want to "top" 24, which factors are possibilities?* As students consider various alternatives, they also multiply several

Table Topper Game Board

1	2	3	4	5	6	7	8	9
2	4	6	8	10	12	14	16	18
3	6	9	12	15	18	21	24	27
4	8	12	16	20	24	28	32	36
5	10	15	20	25	30	35	40	45
6	12	18	24	30	36	42	48	54
7	14	21	28	35	42	49	56	63
8	16	24	32	40	48	56	64	72
9	18	27	36	45	54	63	72	81

combinations of factors. Also, if appropriate, the game board can be reduced to focus on the least or most challenging facts (Dacey, Lynch, and Salemi 2013).

Math Focus

› Gaining fluency with multiplication facts
› Identifying several factor pairs for the same multiple

Materials Needed

› 1 die per group of players
› 2 large paper clips per group
› 1 *Table Topper* Game Board per group (page A-31)
› Optional: 1 *Table Topper* Directions per group (page A-32)

Directions

Goal: Multiply factors to get four products in a row, column, or diagonal on the game board.

› Choose which team will use *X*'s and which will use *O*'s.
› For the first round of play, the opposing team puts a paper clip on one of the factors 1–9, shown at the bottom of the game board. Then the team that is playing first also places its clip on one of the factors. (It may be the same number chosen by the other team or a different number.) The playing team multiplies these two numbers, finds their product in the multiplication table, and "tops" it by writing its symbol, *X* or *O*, on it.
› After this first round, teams alternate turns. On each turn, the playing team moves *either one* of the paper clips to a new factor, multiplies these factors, and writes *X* or *O* on top of the product.
› The first team to have four *X*'s or *O*'s beside each other in a row, column, or diagonal wins.

How It Looks in the Classroom

A third-grade teacher introduces this game once her students have an understanding of multiplication, have developed useful fact strategies, and are working toward fact mastery. She learned the game from some fourth- and fifth-grade teachers who wanted to use the game as a way to keep facts current while students were engaged in strategic thinking. She begins by asking, "What two factors have a product of eighteen?" Her students are not at a stage where they immediately identify all of the factors; one student suggests three times six, while another identifies two times nine. She is not looking for a complete list, but she wants to make sure they recognize that there is more than one option.

The teacher displays the game board, divides the class into two teams (those on the right and those on the left), and appoints a leader for each team. The leaders roll a die to determine which team will go first. She turns to the team with the lesser number and says,

"You may choose any one of the numbers on this factor list." The team decides on the 2 and the teacher directs the leader to place a paper clip on the bottom edge of the paper on top of the 2. The other team, after some discussion, decides to place its paper clip on the 9. Then the team multiplies the two numbers, and the leader writes an X on 18.

The teacher explains that the goal of the game is to get four of their X's or O's in a row, column, or diagonal. Then the other team moves one of the clips, multiplies the factors, and marks an O on the product. The class plays a few more rounds to be sure students understand the directions, and then teams are organized to play among themselves.

Tips from the Classroom

❭ Some students may make choices based on facts they know, rather than on identifying the most strategic factor combinations. Before students move their clip, ask: *What product would help you the most right now?*

❭ You may want to make sticky notes available at each game location. When you hear an interesting fact strategy, ask the student to note it. After the game, post all of the notes on a bulletin board with the heading "Our Fact Strategies."

❭ It can be challenging to decide what to do when students identify a product that is incorrect. We found that some students agreed that a team should lose its turn if it miscalculated a product; some allowed the opponent to decide whether the X or O was written on the correct or incorrect product; and some allowed teams to decide among themselves how to handle this situation.

What to Look For

❭ What strategies do students use when they lack recall of facts?

❭ What facts cause the greatest difficulty for a particular student or group of students?

❭ What evidence is there that players are considering several options when it is their turn?

❭ Do some students limit their play to a specific area of the board?

Variations

❭ Change the game board so that it shows only the factors 1 through 5 and their products.

❭ Change the game board so that it shows only the factors 5 through 9 and their products.

❭ Provide practice with multiplication of multiples of ten by adding a second row of factors at the bottom of the board (10, 20, 30, 40, 50, 60, 70, 80, and 90), and adding a 0 to each multiple on the board. Players choose one factor from the single-digit factors and one from the multiples of ten, and then find the product in the table.

❯ Provide practice with multiplication of decimal numbers by adding a second row of factors at the bottom of the board (0.1, 0.2, 0.3, 0.4, 0.5, 0.6, 0.7, 0.8, 0.9), and changing the multiples on the board to decimals accordingly (for example, change 4 to 0.4). Players choose one factor from the single-digit factors and one from the decimal numbers, and then find their product on the board.

Exit Card Choices

❯ What are all the factor pairs for twenty-four?
❯ If your team was playing first and your opponents put their paper clip on 6, where would you place your clip? Why?
❯ Why might a team like to place its first *X* or *O* on 21?

Figure 5.1 shows a response to the last exit card. Even though earlier in the year these students had done activities involving making different possible rectangles with the same area, for example, 24 square units, they seemed surprised that some products on this game board had more factor pairs than others. They had not analyzed the board before they chose initial products to top, but after responding to this question, one team member said, "We really need to think about this when we play again. I hope we can play tomorrow."

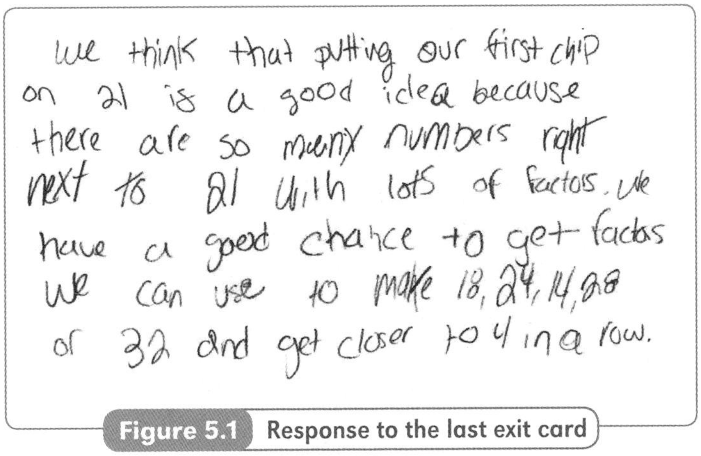

we think that putting our first chip
on 21 is a good idea because
there are so many numbers right
next to 21 with lots of factors. We
have a good chance to get factors
we can use to make 18, 24, 14, 28
or 32 and get closer to 4 in a row.

Figure 5.1 Response to the last exit card

Extension

Use the game as an opportunity for students to reflect on their multiplication fact knowledge, perhaps by completing a table with the headings Facts I Know for Sure, Facts I Am Working On, and Facts I Don't Know. Then use such data to differentiate practice.

Five of a Kind

Why This Game or Puzzle?

It is often easier to identify a missing factor in a format such as $9 \times \underline{\quad} = 36$ than to recognize the same relationship expressed in the division format, such as $36 \div 9 = \underline{\quad}$ (Mauro, LeFevre, and Morris 2003). To identify that 48 divided by 6 is 8, many adults still think, *What times 6 is 48?*

We've taken a game we learned from Michael Schiro (2009) and adapted it to emphasize the important relationships between multiplication and division, as well as provide practice. The goal of the game is to get five cards with equations (at the basic fact level) that have the same missing factor. We've included two sets of cards in the game, one written in the form of missing factors and the other in missing quotients. There are seven matching missing factors or quotients in each set. Playing the same game

Five of a Kind **Factor Cards**

$8 \times \underline{\quad} = 48$	$3 \times \underline{\quad} = 18$
$9 \times \underline{\quad} = 54$	$4 \times \underline{\quad} = 24$
$3 \times \underline{\quad} = 21$	$5 \times \underline{\quad} = 30$
$4 \times \underline{\quad} = 28$	$6 \times \underline{\quad} = 36$
$5 \times \underline{\quad} = 35$	$7 \times \underline{\quad} = 42$

with the two different card formats supports students' understanding of the relationship between multiplication and division.

Math Focus

› Relating multiplication and division
› Dividing or finding missing factors up to 100

Materials Needed

› 1 deck of *Five of a Kind* Factor or Quotient Cards, made from five cards with the same missing factor per group of four players (pages A-33–A-35 or pages A-36–A-38)
› Optional: 1 *Five of a Kind* Directions per group (page A-39)

Directions

Goal: Collect five playing cards with equations that have the same missing factor.

> Four players sit in a circle.
> Sort the cards by putting cards with the same missing factor (or quotient) in the same pile. Choose five cards from each pile to use in the game. Put the other cards aside.
> Shuffle the cards.
> Deal five cards to each player.
> At the same time, each player looks at his or her own cards and decides on one card the player does not want. The player places that card facedown in front of the player to the right. All the players pick up their new cards so that each person once again has five cards in his or her hand.
> Players continue to pass and pick up cards, waiting for all players to pick up before the next pass begins.
> The first player to get five cards with equations that have the same missing factor says, "Five of a kind!" and wins.

How It Looks in the Classroom

One third-grade teacher draws a three-by-five array on the board and asks the students to talk with a partner about the multiplication or division equations the array represents. She tells them to record their ideas. The teacher circles the room as the students talk. She observes that some pairs write only multiplication equations, some pairs write one multiplication and one division equation, and other pairs write four equations. The teacher asks a few pairs to share one of their sentences and records them below the array (Figure 5.2).

The teacher asks, "Why can both multiplication and division be represented by this array?" There is a pause and then Maddy says, "I think it is because they are the same, but sort of backwards. They all use the same numbers."

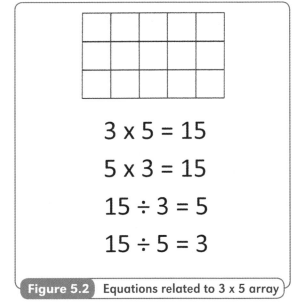

$$3 \times 5 = 15$$
$$5 \times 3 = 15$$
$$15 \div 3 = 5$$
$$15 \div 5 = 3$$

Figure 5.2 Equations related to 3 x 5 array

Craig builds on Maddy's thinking when he says, "I agree with Maddy. When you start with three times five, you have the lengths of the sides and it gets filled in. That's the total. When you start with fifteen, you are starting with the total and one of the sides. You have to find what the length of the other side would be to get that total."

Then the teacher writes $3 \times \underline{\quad} = 12$ on the board and asks what factor is missing. Juliette explains, "It's four, because three times four is twelve."

When the class agrees, the teacher writes 12 ÷ 3 = ____. No one answers quickly, and then Chris says, "Maybe, ask three times what number is twelve? I know that three times four is twelve, so the missing factor is four, but I'm not sure."

Macie says, "I always think about multiplication to help me divide."

The teacher knows that the students need to think about these ideas some more and that this game will help them do so. She organizes them in teams of four and gives each team a deck made from the Factor Cards. To familiarize them with the cards, she tells students to shuffle them and organize them by their missing factors. "But first," she says, "decide how you will work together to sort them." She notes that some groups give everyone a few cards to sort while some work together, one card at a time. A couple of groups take quite a bit of time to decide how to accomplish the sorting process. She is reminded of the need to give students frequent opportunities to decide how they will cooperate to complete a task.

Once all the cards are sorted, she asks them how they found the missing numbers. Juliette summarizes the conversation by saying, "I want to use the fact I know. So for something like 4 × ____ = 16. I think *What times four is sixteen?* For 2 × ___ = 14, I think *What times two is fourteen?*" The teacher then tells the groups to take five cards from each pile they sorted, shuffle these cards for the game, and put the other cards aside. She explains the rules of the game, and play begins.

Tips from the Classroom

〉 To keep the timing of the card passing in sync, you may want to have a player in each group say, "Pass," and "Pick up," as appropriate.

〉 You may wish to allow some students to play with a multiplication table available for reference.

〉 Some students really like games that involve speed along with competition. If you want such students to slow down, consider introducing the cooperative version described in "Variations."

What to Look For

〉 Do students recognize inverse relationships?

〉 How do students determine the missing numbers?

〉 Do players make good choices when they pass cards? That is, do they pass a card without a match or with fewer matches than other cards they have in their hands?

〉 Do students make connections between multiplication and division when playing with the Quotient Cards?

Variations

〉 Differentiate, as needed, by choosing which facts should be included in the deck.

〉 Use fewer cards for each matching missing number and have students collect three or four of a kind to win.

》 Increase the cards included for play and have students collect six or seven of a kind in order to win.

》 Play with a combination from the two decks of cards, making sure there are four to six matches for each missing factor or quotient.

》 Have students play cooperatively. Hands of cards stay faceup for all to see throughout the game. There is no talking allowed in the game. The goal is to have everyone get a set of matched cards in the fewest number of passes.

Exit Card Choices

》 How would you rewrite $7 \times$ ___ $= 42$ as a division problem?

》 What mathematics might you use to find $42 \div 6$, if you couldn't remember this quotient?

》 How can this game help you learn your division facts?

Extension

Create a fact strategy board where students post ideas for finding products and quotients. Such ideas could be general, like *Think multiplication to find quotients*, or specific, such as *Think 5, 6, 7, 8 to remember that 56 ÷ 7 = 8*.

Adapted from *Pass It* in *Mega-fun Math Games and Puzzles for the Elementary Grades* by Michael S. Schiro (San Francisco: Jossey-Bass, 2009).

 **Equal Values**

Why This Game or Puzzle?

This game requires students to identify two multiplication expressions that have the same value. The expressions in the game emphasize the properties of multiplication. Students usually learn these properties when working with single-digit numbers. The distributive property allows students to build on facts they know, for example, thinking of 4×8 as the same as $2 \times 8 + 2 \times 8$. Learners might also find 8×7 by thinking about $10 \times 7 - 2 \times 7$. The commutative property is also helpful, as students may be able to find 9×3 by thinking of 3×9. Later, to generalize the properties, students must also apply them to numbers greater than nine. We also want students to learn that grouping factors in different ways (using the associative property of multiplication) can make it possible to use mental computation to find products of single-digit numbers and multiples of tens and hundreds; for example, it is helpful to multiply 5×2 first to find $45 \times 5 \times 2$.

After finding two expressions that are equal, students are asked to record the expression on each card on either side of an equal sign. Many students misinterpret the equal sign (Ginsberg and Ertle 2008), often construing it to mean "write your answer here." Students may also assume that only one number can be written to its right. Recording pairs of expressions provides students with counterexamples to these assumptions and also provides a list from which patterns and generalizations can be discussed.

Equal Values Cards	
=	=
3×8	8×3
8×7	$5 \times 7 + 3 \times 7$
$6 \times 2 \times 5$	6×10
$4 \times 3 + 4 \times 3$	8×3
9×6	$10 \times 6 - 6$
9×8	8×9
$2 \times 7 + 3 \times 7$	5×7

Math Focus

- Recognizing expressions with products that have the same value
- Applying properties of multiplication
- Multiplying one-, two-, and three-digit numbers

Materials Needed

- 1 deck of *Equal Values* Cards per group of four students (pages A-40–A-42)
- 1 *Equal Values* Recording Sheet per group (page A-43)
- Optional: 1 *Equal Values* Directions per group (page A-44)
- Optional: 1 calculator

Directions

Goal: Get more pairs of cards that have equal values.

- Give each team a card with the equal sign.
- Shuffle the cards. Deal each team four cards faceup for all to see. Put the other cards facedown in a pile.
- On each turn you can do one of three things:
  1. Find two of your cards that have an equal value. Set this pack beside you. Replace them with two cards from the top of the pile.

2. Trade one of your cards with one of the other team's cards when you are able to make a pack. Set this pack beside you. Replace your card with a card from the top of the pile.

3. Draw a card from the top of the pile and add it to your cards.

‣ When a pack is made, both teams must agree on the product and then one player records their thinking.

‣ If no cards are left in the deck, you can still have a turn, but you don't take a card.

‣ The game ends when no team can make another pack.

‣ The team with more packs wins.

How It Looks in the Classroom

One teacher writes the following list of expressions on the board and asks students to work with a partner to find two expressions that have the same value.

$$4 \times 37$$
$$30 \times 4 + 7 \times 4$$
$$2 \times 37 + 2 \times 37$$
$$37 \times 4$$

Keather and Joe work together. When it is time to share thinking with the larger groups, Keather identifies the first and last expressions as having the same values. Joe then explains, "You can change the order of the numbers." The teacher asks what those numbers are called, and Keather identifies the term *factors*.

Peter selects the first two expressions in the list and says, "Because you can split the factors."

Shakira says, "Wait, if the first one is the same as the second one and the last one, then all three must be equal."

Bryon is excited by this idea and suggests that all four expressions have the same value. The teacher divides the class into four sections and assigns each group one of the four expressions to compute, to prove or disprove Bryon's thinking. Once the products are all reported to be 148, the teacher asks them how they might recognize that the expressions would have the same value. The students decide that expressions that split one of the numbers using the distributive property or expressions that change the order of the factors will be the same.

The teacher explains that their thinking will help them to play *Equal Values* and projects the rules of the game. After reading the directions and having two teams model the game for the larger group, students play the game in groups of four.

Tips from the Classroom

〉 At first we were uncertain as to whether students should stop play to record their matching expressions. Through field-testing we found that it did slow down the game, but that the slower pace encouraged attention to whether or not the expressions were equivalent. A game may require two recording sheets.

〉 You may wish to make the equal signs on paper stock of a different color or cut off the white space around them, so they don't get lost among the other cards.

〉 Encourage students who are unsure whether two expressions are equal or not to replace the larger numbers with smaller ones and see what they think. This approach is an example of simplifying a problem, an important problem-solving strategy.

〉 You may want some students to use calculators to check the products so that the multiplication does not make the game tedious.

What to Look For

〉 What strategies do students use to find equal products?

〉 Do students recognize examples of the commutative, associative, or distributive properties?

〉 What language do students use when deciding whether two expressions are equal or not?

〉 Do players consider what cards their opponents have when they decide which card to give away?

Variations

〉 For third-grade students, make more examples of cards similar to those on page A-40.

〉 For a greater challenge, use only the cards on pages A-41 and A-42.

〉 Play with division expressions and then with both multiplication and division expressions, allowing students to note inverse relationships such as 30×3 and $90 \div 3$.

Exit Card Choices

〉 How do you know that $7 \times 63 = 63 \times 7$?

〉 What are some different ways you could find 27×6?

〉 What two expressions can you write that are equal to 5×92?

Extension

Post several expressions throughout the room and have a scavenger hunt. Teams can use the *Equal Values* Recording Sheet (page A-43) to record those they find with the same value.

Game adapted from an unpublished game created by Suzanne Lak, a Cambridge public school educator.

Think Remainder

Why This Game or Puzzle?

Addition, subtraction, and multiplication with whole numbers all result in answers that are also whole numbers, with no leftover parts. Division is different in this way. In fact, given random numbers, division would be more likely to result in a quotient with a remainder than in a whole number quotient. For example, among the numbers one through fifty, more numbers would have a remainder when divided by five than would not. Remainders are just one aspect of division that makes this operation what many consider to be the most complex algorithm of the basic four operations (Back 2013).

As number sense develops, students begin to recognize which division examples will and will not have a remainder. For example, most students quickly recognize numbers divisible by two or five. In this game, one team rolls a die to identify the divisor and then the opposing team chooses a number for the dividend from the numbers on the game board. The team that rolled divides to find the quotient, and the remainder identifies the number of points that team receives. The team with the higher score wins the game. This scoring structure encourages the opposing team to choose the dividend carefully, allowing for both teams to participate in each team's turn.

Think Remainder Game Board

11	12	13	15
17	18	19	20
21	23	24	27
29	31	32	35
42	44	47	49

Math Focus

› Computing quotients with remainders
› Understanding relationships among divisors, dividend, quotients, and remainders

Materials Needed

› 1 die per group of players
› 1 *Think Remainder* Game Board per group (page A-45)
› 1 *Think Remainder* Recording Sheet per team (page A-46)
› Optional: 1 *Think Remainder* Directions per group (page A-47)

Directions

Goal: Have the greater sum when adding the remainders of ten division examples.

› Take turns. When it's your team's turn, your team is known as the "rolling team."
› A member of the rolling team rolls the die.
› A member of the opposing team crosses out a number on the game board.
› Players on the rolling team divide the number crossed out by the number rolled. The remainder is the rolling team's score for this turn. A member of the team records the numbers for this turn on the team's recording sheet.
› Teams take turns rolling, crossing out numbers, dividing, and recording the work for this turn. (Crossed-out numbers cannot be used again.)
› When every number on the board has been crossed out, teams compare their total scores by adding all the remainders from their turns.
› The team with the greater score wins.

How It Looks in the Classroom

One fifth-grade teacher introduces the game by displaying the following numbers: 24, 37, 45, 57, 59. The teacher divides the class into two teams and asks a student on the left side of the room to roll a die. The student announces that she rolled a 6. The teacher tells students on the other side of the room to pick one of the numbers on the board, explaining that the other team will have to find the quotient, and the remainder will be the number of points that team receives. After a quick discussion, a student reports, "We'll choose fifty-nine so that they have to use the biggest number." There is a groan when it is determined that their opponents will get 5 points.

The teacher says, "Take a minute to talk with your neighbor about related number facts that could help you decide whether fifty-nine was a good choice for six." There is slight pause before the conversation begins, but when it does, students start recognizing that thinking about both $54 \div 6$ and $60 \div 6$ would be helpful.

The class plays another round, giving the other team the opportunity to earn points. The team rolls a 3 and the opposing team chooses forty-five. When asked why the team made this choice, Alesia and David take turns explaining that they split forty-five into thirty and fifteen, and because both of these numbers are multiples of three, they knew the rolling team would get 0 points.

The teacher then asks the students to summarize the rules of the game before they play on their own.

Tips from the Classroom

〉 In our field testing, some opposing teams wanted to complete several division examples, using paper and pencil, before choosing the dividend. Be clear that teams must choose dividends without using paper-and-pencil computation.

〉 Opposing teams quickly recognize that when a 1 is rolled, they can choose any number on the board and the rolling team will get a score of 0. This recognition can sometimes help the game move along quickly, which works well. Once skills increase, you can decide to have the 1 stand for another number, such as 7 or 8.

What to Look For

〉 Do students make random choices or consider the potential outcomes of several choices they could make?

〉 What evidence do you see that students recognize that choosing a multiple of the number rolled will result in a score of 0?

〉 What strategies do students use to find quotients once both numbers are chosen? Do they rely on related multiplication or division facts?

〉 What generalizations do students make about divisors, dividends, quotients, and remainders?

Variations

〉 The game can be made more or less challenging by changing the numbers on the *Think Remainder* Game Board.

〉 Polyhedral dice or spinners could be used if you want students to have a greater number of divisors to work with.

〉 You could make turns more traditional by allowing each team to roll the die, choose the number on the game board, and then compute its score.

〉 You could allow for use of calculators, requiring students to figure out how to determine the whole number remainder once they identify a quotient.

Exit Card Choices

〉 When it's your turn to cross out a number, how does the number rolled help you decide the number to cross out? Give examples.

〉 Why might the number 24 be crossed out early in the game?

〉 What number would you like to roll? Why?

A response to the first exit card is shown in Figure 5.3. The students on this team appeared to choose somewhat randomly in the first two turns, but in the third round, one of the players said, "Wait, we could make a really good choice." They were quite excited when they realized that when a 1 was rolled, their choice was easy. After playing two games, they had developed their strategy for choosing numbers to cross out.

We really like it when a 1 is called because then we can pick anything. It's like a free turn! For a 2 we go for an even number. For the other numbers we look for multiples. If they are all gone, we look for numbers close to multiples.

Figure 5.3 Response to the first exit card

Extension

Some students may want to learn about divisibility rules. Students will be able to create rules for several numbers by looking at patterns. Those who wish to learn more about such rules could investigate online references such as https://www.mathsisfun.com/divisibility-rules.html.

Matchups

Why This Game or Puzzle?

Robert Fisher (2005) argues that the focus of teaching should be on helping students learn how to gain, organize, and use information. Puzzles often require such skills. Possible alternatives must be identified and then investigated. Solvers must make choices that enable them to meet all criteria.

For this puzzle, solvers must write each of the listed factors below exactly one of its listed multiples. Students must do so in such a way that each factor is used exactly once and each multiple is matched with one and only one of its factors. Thus, solvers must consider which numbers have a factor-multiple relationship, perhaps making lists and then eliminating possibilities as the solving continues. Strategic thinkers may try to narrow the decision space by first identifying multiples and factors that must be matched because there is only one choice for them. Solvers may also notice patterns that allow them to make generalizations such as *If it is a multiple of six, it is also a multiple of two and three.* As such, this puzzle offers opportunities for students to apply a variety of problem-solving strategies while deepening their number sense and practicing their multiplication and division skills.

Two versions of the puzzle are provided; Puzzle B is more challenging than Puzzle A.

Math Focus

› Identifying factors and multiples
› Finding patterns and making generalizations

Matchups Puzzle A

Name(s): _____ Date: _____

Write each factor below one of its multiples. The factor cannot be the same number as the multiple you choose. You must write each factor exactly once and write a number on each line.

Factor List

1	2	3	5	7
8	9	10	25	

Multiple Board

11	80	45
32	15	21
50	4	10

Materials Needed

› 1 *Matchups* Puzzle A or B per pair of students (page A-48 or A-49)
› Optional: 1 *Matchups* Directions per pair (page A-50)

Directions

Goal: Using each factor only once, match each given factor with exactly one given multiple.

› Each number in the factor list is a factor of one or more of the numbers on the multiple board.
› Write each factor on a blank beneath one of its multiples on the board. The factor cannot be the same number as the multiple you choose. Each factor must be written exactly once.
› Write the factors so that each multiple gets a match.

How Does It Work?

Though conversations with partners tend to be informal, this fourth-grade teacher knows that developing familiarity with mathematical terms is important. She decides to review some vocabulary that students might incorporate into their discussion of this puzzle during the solution process or into a class discussion after everyone has solved the puzzle. She gathers the students in the meeting area and announces that they are going to review some mathematical terms by dramatizing them. She says, "You are going to make a scene, using just your actions, without any talking or any props, to help us to know the term you are identifying. For example, what scene might you create for *addition*?"

Judi suggests, "We could show two collections of chips and then push them together and point at them as if we are counting. Oh, wait, we can't use props."

David says, "We could just put us in two groups and motion us together."

The teacher then reveals the list of words written on chart paper: *square number, even number, multiple, factor, prime number*. "Join your neighbors in groups of three or four, making sure everyone near you has partners. Then talk about what these words mean and how you could dramatize them. You need to show the meanings of the terms, not just examples."

While the students talk, the teacher moves from group to group, making sure students understand the terms and encouraging their creativity. She is not surprised that students' initial thoughts are to show numbers with their fingers, for example, by putting up two, four, six, eight, and ten fingers for even numbers. She reminds them to focus on why we identify these numbers as even.

After about ten minutes, the groups come back together and share their ideas. There is great energy in the room as they build on others' thinking. For example, they all agree that it is challenging to distinguish a scene for factors from one for multiples. Together, they decide to have one student circle her arms around two others, with those encircled waving their hands for *factor* and the one student rocking back and forth for *multiple*. A few students dramatize the scene, taking care to give emphasis to the role of factor or multiple, depending on the intention. For prime numbers they decide to have a line of students walk to an identified spot, but only two of them are allowed to stay. These two students send the others away by shaking their heads and raising their hands to a stop position.

The teacher is pleased with their engagement and dramatic flair. She believes that integration with the arts leads to greater retention. She asks the students to reflect on what they learned and there is general agreement that they enjoyed the activity and that it helped them remember the terms. She then announces that they are going to do a puzzle in which they may find themselves talking with their partners about some of these same ideas.

The teacher displays the puzzle (Puzzle B in this case) and reviews the directions. She asks, "Who can tell me where the 10 might be written?"

Jasmine responds, "You could write it under the 310, 100, 700, 150, and 70."

Dani asks, "But how will we know where to write it?"

The answers vary. A few students suggest it could be written under any of these multiples, and others agree with Chan, who states, "It depends. You have to do more of the puzzle to know."

Satisfied that they are ready, the teacher distributes copies of the puzzle along with the invitation to "Start puzzling."

Tips from the Classroom

> Most students began by making random choices and then realized that their choices were not going to allow them to match each multiple. As they persevered, they began to make lists or to recognize numbers with fewer factor choices (such as 13) or factors with limited choices of multiples (such as 31).

> A few students got frustrated with the number of times they had to erase. It helped them to write the factors on discs that they could move around as they considered alternatives.

❯ Some students may ask to use a calculator to identify all of the factors of each multiple. Encourage such students to first see if they can identify some numbers that must match. We found that once students experienced some success, they became engaged in the puzzle and no longer asked for calculators.

What to Look For

❯ What language do students use to describe their thinking? Do they refer to *square*, *prime*, or *even* numbers? Do they use the terms *factor* and *multiple*?

❯ What problem-solving strategies do students use? Do they make lists? Guess and check?

❯ Are there particular factors your students have difficulty deciding where to place?

❯ What computation strategies do students use to determine whether a number is a factor of a particular multiple?

Variations

❯ You can create puzzles of different levels of challenge by using more obvious or less obvious factor-multiple relationships. Including one prime number is helpful as well as numbers that have few factors, such as twenty-five and forty-nine.

❯ This puzzle could also be a game. Create a card for each factor. To play the game, students deal all the cards, and on each turn a player places a factor on one of its multiples on the shared multiple board. Only one card may be placed on each multiple. Players alternate turns. The game ends when a player cannot place a card. The player with the fewest cards left in his or her hand wins.

Exit Card Choices

❯ Which multiple has only one matching factor on the list?

❯ Which number on the multiple board has the most factors listed on the factor list?

❯ What problem-solving strategies did you use to complete this puzzle? Give an example of how these strategies helped you make one of the matches.

Extension

Have students list the numbers 1 through 30 and all of their factors, including improper factors; for example, 8: 1, 2, 4, and 8. Encourage students to notice patterns and make generalizations. Possible observations include the following: square numbers have an odd number of factors; prime numbers have exactly two factors; and two is the only even number with exactly two factors.

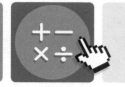

Online Games and Apps

As with addition and subtraction, there is a plethora of online games and apps for practicing the basic facts of multiplication and division. Such games and activities give students an opportunity to practice in an often engaging environment and provide an interesting alternative to flash cards and timed tests.

While not as readily available online as fact-based games, there are games that require students to employ a conceptual understanding of multiplication or division to complete a task or to think strategically about the use of the algorithm. Such games are often set in high-energy, engaging contexts that focus on an end goal or have solving a puzzle as the primary purpose. Following are some examples:

- Pick-a-Path, a free game found on the Illuminations website of the National Council of Teachers of Mathematics (NCTM) at http://illuminations.nctm.org/pickapath, requires students to navigate through a series of paths with an engaging character, Okta the octopus. Players must compute multiplication and division problems while winding their way through the various paths from top to bottom, attempting to obtain the highest or lowest possible total or reach a specific value, considered the target for that round of play. Players must try to choose the correct path to reach the target, with some game boards offering several alternatives. Levels 1–3 focus on using whole numbers and factors and powers of ten, while levels 4–7 engage students in the use of fractions, decimals, measurement, and exponents.

- Factor Dazzle, one of a number of free games and activities found on the NCTM-supported website Calculation Nation (go to https://calculationnation.nctm.org/ and click on "Play Games"), allows students to play against an individual or a team to find factors of a chosen number on a game board. One team chooses a number on the board and the opposing team chooses all of the available factors on the board. The totals of the numbers chosen during one turn become the scores for each team. The opposing team then chooses the starting number while the first team chooses factors, realizing that, as play continues, the previously chosen numbers are no longer available. Students who recognize the difference between numbers with many factors and those with few factors will begin to informally define such number concepts as prime and composite numbers. Strategic play gives students the opportunity to think about what makes for a good (or less desirable) first move, what numbers will produce the best score, and whether there is a way to always win based on appropriate moves. Such ideas can provide a focus for classroom discussion or serve as exit card questions to assess students' understanding.

- Break Apart, one of a number of free games in the Greg Tang games suite (go to http://www.gregtangmath.com/games) requires students to solve a multiplication or division problem using a specified break-apart strategy. Usually playing alone or in pairs, students work toward the goal of finding the answers in the shortest time possible. The player is directly learning to compute more efficiently using strategies such as finding an answer to a problem involving six as a factor by thinking of two groups with three as a factor. The concept of partial quotients is introduced by visually displaying breaking the division problem into two problems with smaller divisors. For example, $108 \div 6$ is displayed as $60 \div 6$ and $48 \div 6$. As well as the visual displays, an added benefit of the online technology is evident in the varied strategy choices students are given.

Mixed Operations

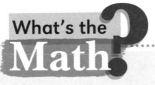

What's the Math?

Sharon Griffin (2004) suggests that teaching with a focus on conceptual relationships, rather than procedural rules, supports students' number sense. Games and puzzles involving mixed operations provide opportunities for students to further investigate relationships among operations and numbers. For example, through experimentation and discussion, students can develop the ability to understand that if $20 \times 5 - 1 = 99$, then $20 \times 5 + 1 = 101$, without actually computing. They begin to recognize that by adding instead of subtracting the 1, the total value increases by two. Students can also gain operational sense. For example, if the numbers 3, 5, and 9 are to be used in an expression equal to 32, students will recognize that multiplication must be involved in some way.

Lins and Kaput encourage teachers to introduce students to algebraic ways of thinking prior to middle school to "immerse them in the *culture of algebra*" (2004, 48). Such a culture involves thinking about relationships (often referred to as relational thinking) like those described above. It also allows students to experience mathematics through sense-making activities. Students make and test conjectures; they look for and generalize patterns. Students might notice, for example, that all multiples of four are even numbers and decide to investigate multiples of six and eight or think about how this relates to their observation that the sum of even numbers is always even. Looking for relationships, patterns, and generalizations helps students build a bridge between arithmetic and algebraic thinking while deepening their conceptual understanding and strengthening or maintaining their procedural skills.

Another mathematical aspect of working with mixed operations is the order in which we calculate. Though the order of operations is often introduced in fourth grade, many third graders have access to calculators, perhaps on a phone, which automatically apply this order, so knowledge of this convention is useful in the real world. Just giving students the rule is not enough; it should be developed in conjunction with their experiences (Golembo 2000). When a student is playing a game or solving a puzzle involving mixed operations, he might describe his steps by saying, "I multiplied 3 times 6 and then I subtracted 18 from 20 and divided by 2 to get 1." Such examples lend themselves to the investigation of how the process should be represented in an equation; in this case it would be $(20 - 3 \times 6) \div 2 = 1$.

Finally, in school math, we tend to link addition and subtraction together, as well as multiplication and division. There is also a shorter period of time where we might link addition to multiplication and subtraction to division. This coupling limits students' choice of operations much too frequently. In everyday life, we use any combination of the four basic operations as appropriate. Games and puzzles with mixed operations allow learners to consider all operations and decide which are appropriate in a given situation.

Roll Six

Why This Game or Puzzle?
Using relational thinking to solve number sentences involves important aspects of mathematical thinking such as equivalence and compensation (Carpenter, Franke, and Levi 2003). Such thinking allows us to use mental arithmetic to find 99×2 by recognizing its relationship to 100×2 and then compensating for the difference between the two expressions by subtracting: $99 \times 2 = 100 \times 2 - 2 = 198$.

In the beginning of this game, players roll a die and find products involving the factors one through six. Then, players try to use these products to return to the numbers one through six, that is, to create expressions equal to each of these goal numbers. The proximity of these numbers may make it useful for players to use relational thinking and consider whether expressions from one example could be altered to equal another needed outcome.

Math Focus

› Finding sums, differences, products, and quotients
› Creating expressions for given values
› Looking for patterns and relationships among equations

Roll Six Recording Sheet

Name(s): _____   Date: _____

	Rolled	Product
1		
2		
3		
4		
5		
6		

Use the products to complete the equations. A product may be used only once in a particular equation. Not all of the products must be included in each equation.

_____ = 1
_____ = 2
_____ = 3
_____ = 4
_____ = 5
_____ = 6

You score 1 point for each equation that is recorded accurately.

Score: _____

Materials Needed

› 1 die per group of players
› 1 three-minute timer per group
› 1 *Roll Six* Recording Sheet per team (page A-51)
› Optional: 1 *Roll Six* Directions per group (page A-52)

Directions

Goal: Roll numbers on a die, use them in a table to find products, and then use the products to write expressions equal to each of the numbers one through six.

› For the first part of the game, opponents work together to complete the table at the top of their recording sheets. To begin, a player on one team rolls the die and that team decides where, in the second column of the table, the number will be recorded. Both teams then record the number and the product of the two numbers in that row. For example, if the team rolls a 6 and places it in the column beside the 2, it records 12 in the third column.

› Teams take turns rolling and deciding where the number will be recorded until the table is completed.

› Next, a player starts the timer and teams have three minutes to use these products to privately create equations with the values 1 through 6. So if the players have the products 3, 8, 18, 20, 5, and 36, then each team uses these numbers to complete equations with values of 1, 2, 3, 4, 5, and 6. A product may not be used more than once in a single equation. Not all of the products have to be included in each equation.

> › When the time is up, teams share their equations and check each other's work for accuracy. Teams get a point for each of the numbers one through six for which they could write an accurate equation. The team with the greater number of points wins. (If each team gets the same number of points, it is a tie.)

How It Looks in the Classroom

One third-grade teacher poses a "do now" task as students enter the classroom, so that he can refer to it later in the day when he introduces the game. The task is shown in Figure 6.1.

Use some or all of these numbers once in each equation: 24, 15, 9, 4, 6, 12. What different equations can you write with a value equal to 5?

Figure 6.1 "Do now" task

Note that he has purposely chosen numbers that occur in this game and a value for which everyone is likely to find at least one example, that is, $9 - 4 = 5$. When a student suggests the equation $15 - 6 \div 9 + 4 = 5$, it is an opportunity to discuss the need for parentheses to indicate that you want to subtract before you divide.

Later that morning, he gathers students in the rug area, where he has projected the *Roll Six* Recording Sheet for all to see. He gives pairs of students a copy of the sheet. He divides the group in half and invites Nicole to represent her team on the right side of the room. He tells her to roll a die and then talk with her team about where to write the number she rolls in the table at the top of the recording sheet. (The teacher knows that the choice is random at this early stage of learning the game but wants to reinforce the idea of teams working together.) Nicole rolls a 5 and her team decides to write the number in the Roll column beside the 3. The teacher records the 5 and asks all the students to do so as well. The students readily identify 15 as the product, and the teacher and the students record this number in the last column.

Next, Miguel is invited to roll for the other team and then he, too, consults with his team about where to write the number shown on the die. The class identifies the product of these two numbers and the teacher and students record these results as well. Players from the two teams continue to take turns until the table is complete.

The teacher then asks Haley to remind everyone of the "do now" task from this morning. Once they've reviewed the task, he draws their attention to the second part of the recording sheet, where players are to complete equations. He explains that just as they did this morning, they will use specific numbers to create equations. Here, they will use the products they recorded to create equations equal to the numbers one through six. He tells them they will have three minutes to work with their partners to complete the equations. He sets the timer on his phone and announces, "Begin!"

Tips from the Classroom

❭ Some students tend to incorporate only addition and subtraction. You might ask, *Are there other operations that might be helpful?*

❭ Some students may think the game does not begin until the products are determined and might not realize that the completion of the table is an integral part of the game. For example, having a product of one, or two products with a difference of one, could be helpful when writing equations with similar values. After playing, questions may stimulate some different thinking about the initial stage of the game. For example, you could ask, *What number do you wish you had in your products and why?*

❭ Because teams are working with the same numbers, you may wish to have them work behind upright file folders to preserve the privacy of their choices.

❭ Players show interest in what their opponents have created and do tend to check for accuracy, though you may need to remind a few players of this expectation.

❭ Using a timer can add a level of competition that helps transform a task into a game. Some students are able to accomplish more without the pressure of a time limit. Help students make the choice that is best for them.

❭ We found that many students wanted to play this game again. You may wish to copy the game board on both sides of the paper.

What to Look For

❭ Do you see students using what they know from one equation to help them create a different equation? For example, what evidence of such thinking do you see in the recording sheet shown in Figure 6.2?

❭ How do students communicate the order of the operations in a way that makes sense?

❭ What strategies do you notice that you would like students to share with the larger group?

❭ Do the players on a team work independently and then compare? Do they brainstorm ideas together?

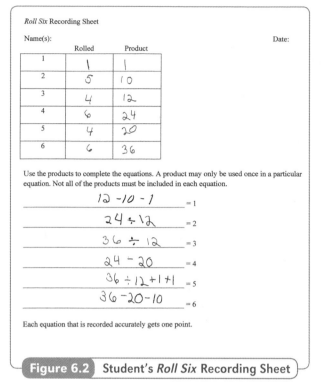

Roll Six Recording Sheet

Name(s): _____   Date: _____

	Rolled	Product
1	1	1
2	5	10
3	4	12
4	6	24
5	4	20
6	6	36

Use the products to complete the equations. A product may only be used once in a particular equation. Not all of the products must be included in each equation.

$$12 - 10 - 1 = 1$$
$$24 \div 12 = 2$$
$$36 \div 12 = 3$$
$$24 - 20 = 4$$
$$36 \div 12 + 1 + 1 = 5$$
$$36 - 20 - 10 = 6$$

Each equation that is recorded accurately gets one point.

Figure 6.2 | Student's *Roll Six* Recording Sheet

Variations

❭ One group of students in the field testing proposed an option for when the time ended and there was a tie. They suggested that players could have extra time to find an equation for any value not yet found, or if they had completed the task, they could have time to find a second, different equation for each value and be awarded one bonus point for each new equation created.

❭ Another group suggested that the game could be untimed and instead end as soon as one team found an equation for each value or end when both teams agreed they were finished because no other equations could be formed.

Exit Card Choices

❭ In the first part of the game, could you get a product of twenty-one to use in your equations? Explain.

❭ Players on one team said they could not write equations for the odd numbers 1, 3, and 5 because all of the products were even. Are they correct?

❭ What relationships did you notice among the numbers that helped you create more equations?

Extension

Establish an occasional number routine in which you provide four random numbers and students have three minutes to find all the different expressions they can write, each with a different value. Each expression must be formed using at least two of the four numbers, none more than once, and any operations.

Write It Right

Why This Game or Puzzle?

When she was president of the National Council of Teachers of Mathematics, Cathy Seeley wrote, "Algebraic thinking includes recognizing and analyzing patterns, studying and representing relationships, making generalizations, and analyzing how things change" (2004). For *Write It Right* puzzles, solvers must recognize relationships and patterns to place the numbers zero through nine exactly once so that each of four equations is correct. Discussion of solution strategies can lead to students noting properties of arithmetic or forming generalizations. For example, in the first puzzle, students might rely on the zero property of multiplication to recognize where zero is placed, generalize that factors with a product that is an odd number must both be odd, or realize that the sum of any two single-digit numbers is less than nineteen. They might also discover, through investigation, that with factors zero through nine, there is only one product that is a two-digit number ending in three: sixty-three. As students discover such implied information within the equations, their strategic thinking develops, they make lists, and eliminate possibilities.

Three puzzles are provided, so that appropriate choices may be made for your students. Puzzles A and B are limited to whole numbers. Puzzle C includes decimal numbers.

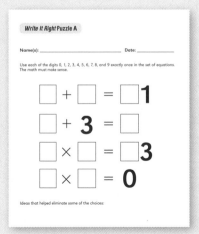

Write It Right Puzzle A

Name(s): _____ Date: _____

Use each of the digits 0, 1, 2, 3, 4, 5, 6, 7, 8, and 9 exactly once in the set of equations. The math must make sense.

$$\square + \square = \square\,1$$
$$\square + 3 = \square$$
$$\square \times \square = \square\,3$$
$$\square \times \square = 0$$

Ideas that helped eliminate some of the choices:

Math Focus

› Looking for patterns
› Making generalizations
› Finding sums, differences, products, and quotients

Materials Needed

› 1 *Write It Right* Puzzle A, B, or C per pair of students (page A-53, A-54, or A-55)
› Optional: 1 *Write It Right* Directions per pair (page A-56)

Directions

Goal: Write the given numbers in the puzzle so that all the equations are true.

› Use each of the given numbers exactly once in the puzzle.
› The equations must be true.
› Check to make sure each equation is correct.
› Identify ideas that helped you decide where to write the numbers.

How It Looks in the Classroom

A fourth-grade teacher displays the mini-puzzle shown in Figure 6.3. She tells students to read the puzzle and talk with their neighbors about what it asks them to do. She then asks volunteers to explain the task in their own words. Jadon says, "Each number gets written in a square to make the math work." Next the teacher invites students to work together on the puzzle. She also lets them know that after a brief amount of time, she will ask them to stop and talk as a whole group.

As they work, the teacher notices that most of the students are not talking; they are trying out ideas by writing the numbers in the squares and then usually erasing the numbers because some of their choices do not work. She thinks it is time for them to stop and share what they have learned so far. As she often does when she asks students to share their early thinking, she says, "Remember when we do a quick stop and talk, we talk about our thinking, but don't tell our answers."

Leland says, "I tried 2 plus 3 equals 5, but then I couldn't find anything that worked for the second one, so I tried 3 plus 3 equals 6. But that didn't work either, when I tried the other equations."

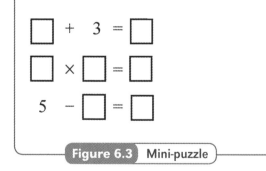

Write the numbers 0, 1, 2, 3, 4, 5, and 6 exactly once.

The equations must be true.

$$\square + 3 = \square$$
$$\square \times \square = \square$$
$$5 - \square = \square$$

Figure 6.3 Mini-puzzle

Johanna says, "I started with the first equation, too. I made a list of all the numbers that would work. I think there's another combination Leland could try."

The teacher would like another approach shared as well, so she asks, "Did anyone start with a different equation?"

Demi says, "I started with the second equation, because I knew only small numbers could be used. First I thought there would be too many choices because 1 would work with all the numbers, but then I realized I couldn't write, like, 2 times 1 is 2, because I only had one 2. Then I found numbers that worked."

The teacher then invites the students to return to their puzzling. When they do, she notices that the students become involved in animated conversations. When she sees that partners have reached a solution to the puzzle, she asks them to jot some notes about their thinking. When the group comes back together, the students agree that the solution is $1 + 3 = 4$; $2 \times 3 = 6$; and $5 - 5 = 0$. The students are enthusiastic about trying another puzzle, so she gives them copies of *Write It Right* Puzzle A, pointing out that this time the numbers zero through nine are included.

Tips from the Classroom

> Most solvers will guess and test a variety of alternatives. Some students found it helpful to write each of the numbers 0 through 9 on a small piece of paper that they could move around as they were evaluating choices. Students can also use erasable markers on laminated puzzle boards.

> For students who need help getting started, you could focus on a particular equation and ask, *What numbers are possible for this equation?* or *What do you know about products in the forties?*

> Some students may need time to look at the puzzle independently before sharing ideas with their partners. We found such sharing helped students remember ideas that eliminated choices.

> It can be challenging to decide when to have students explore, perhaps relying only on trial and error, and when to prod their thinking to be more strategic. We found it helped to have students solve the first puzzle and then discuss their thinking as a large group. After they became more aware of how to eliminate some of their choices, they used such thinking to solve the second puzzle. Regardless of their approaches, students described the puzzles as fun and were proud of their ability to complete them.

> Some students were interested in creating their own versions of the puzzle. It was clear that doing so allowed them to note new patterns and generalizations.

What to Look For

> What conjectures do students make as they guess and test possibilities?

> What ideas do partners talk about that you think should be shared with the larger group?

> Do partners share the responsibility for making choices?

Variations

> You could create simpler puzzles such as the one presented in the "How It Looks in the Classroom" discussion or ones with only two operations, such as addition and multiplication.

> For more challenge, you could create puzzles requiring more complex computation.

Exit Card Choices

❭ Given just the clue □ + □ = 1 □, what do you know?

❭ Which number was the most challenging to place? Why?

❭ Describe two ideas that helped you eliminate some of your choices. Give an example for each.

One teacher gave her students the opportunity to choose which exit card they wished to answer. A common response to the first question was that the two numbers would have to have a sum of ten or greater. One student suggested that at least one of the numbers would have to be five or greater. Another student demonstrated perseverance in problem solving by listing of all the possibilities (see Figure 6.4). She also noticed a pattern in the number of possibilities. As she explained, "I see a pattern that if one number is 1, then there is only one possibility for the other number, and if one number is 2, then there are two possibilities; for 3, there are three possibilities; and this will keep going and maybe some numbers might start repeating. I also know that the numbers can't be small and that is why only 1 and 9 work if 1 is one of the numbers."

This same student decided to consider the third question as well (see Figure 6.5). She notes the zero property of multiplication and limits the possible sum of single-digit numbers to less than eighteen, as the puzzle does not allow for a number to be used more than once, which eliminates nine plus nine.

Extension

These multistep puzzles give students the opportunity to write a mathematical argument for how they found a solution. Have students write a clear and complete explanation. Encourage them to use phrases such as *To find*; *First I*; *Now I know*; *Then I*; and *In conclusion*.

1	9
2	9
2	8
3	9
3	8
3	7
4	9
4	8
4	7
4	6
5	9
5	8
5	7
5	6

Figure 6.4 Student response to first exit question

I knew zero had to be in the last multiplication problem because 0 x anything is zero.

The answer to the first addition problem had to be 11 because you can't add up to 18 with two single digit numbers

Figure 6.5 Student response to third exit question

Decade Roll

Why This Game or Puzzle?

Teachers often give students the mnemonic device *PEMDAS*, which stands for "parentheses, exponents, multiplication, division, addition, and subtraction," or the phrase *Please pity my dear aunt Sally*, which uses a *p* for "powers" rather than *e* for "exponents," as a way to remember the order of operations. Though memory triggers are helpful, both of these are often cited as causing the misconception that, for example, all multiplication must be done before division. Instead, each memory trigger should be thought of in pairs: *p* and *e*, *m* and *d*, and *a* and *s*. These three computations are completed in order, but the computations within the pairs are completed as they occur, left to right. For example, the answer to $18 \div 3 \times 2$ is found by dividing and then multiplying, resulting in the answer 12. Even if students have not yet been taught this convention, you want to make sure they are able to verbally communicate their thinking through language such as *First I found* or through a list of equations showing the order in which they computed.

In this game, players roll four dice and use each of the numbers shown to write expressions equal to a number in each of the decades (ones, tens, twenties, etc.). The numbers rolled can be combined to form multidigit numbers, which increases the number of alternatives to be explored. Along with encouraging relational thinking, this game gives students the opportunity to make sure they are interpreting or communicating the convention for order of operations appropriately and to practice their mental arithmetic.

Decade Roll **Recording Sheet**

Name(s): _____ Date: _____

Numbers rolled: _____ _____ _____ _____

Equations created:

0–9: _____

10–19: _____

20–29: _____

30–39: _____

40–49: _____

50–59: _____

60–69: _____

70–79: _____

80–89: _____

Math Focus

> Finding sums, differences, products, and quotients
> Creating expressions for given values
> Looking for patterns and relationships among equations
> Communicating the order of operations

Materials Needed

› 4 dice per group of players
› 1 two-minute timer per group
› 1 *Decade Roll* Recording Sheet per team (page A-57)
› Optional: 1 *Decade Roll* Directions per group (page A-58)
› Optional: 1 calculator per group

Directions

Goal: Roll dice and use each of the numbers shown to write expressions equal to a number in each of the decades ones through nineties.

› Choose one student to roll four dice.

› Each team has two minutes to privately use the numbers rolled to make expressions that equal numbers in each decade from the ones to the nineties. Each expression must use each of the numbers rolled exactly once. The numbers can be used as single digits or be combined to form two- or three-digit numbers.

› You may use any of the four operations in the equations. More than one operation may be used. So if you rolled dice showing the numbers 4, 5, 1, and 6 and wanted to write an equation for a number in the teens, possibilities would include $4 + 5 + 1 + 6 = 16$; $61 - 45 = 16$; $4 \times 5 - 1 - 6 = 13$; and $5 + 1 \times 6 + 4 = 15$.

› Write the equations on the *Decade Roll* Recording Sheet. Be sure to include parentheses if needed.

› When the time is finished, trade papers, and check each other's equations. The winner is the team with the greater number of correct equations.

How It Looks in the Classroom

One fifth-grade teacher asks students to find the value of the expression $72 \div 8 \times 3 - 2 + 1$. There is a variety of responses, which she records for all to see: *24, 0, 2,* and *26* (correct). The students are quite surprised to see the variety. She asks one of the students who reported twenty-four to use words to describe how he or she found that answer. As she continues this process, she records their comments on chart paper.

› 24: I started with the division and got 9. Nine times 3 is 27, and then you subtract 3, which is 24.

› 0: You multiply first, and 8 times 3 is 24. Then I divided, and 72 divided by 24 is 3. Then 3 minus 3 is 0.

❯ 2: I did the same, except at the end. Three minus 2 is 1. One and 1 is 2.

❯ 26: It's already in the right order, so I just worked left to right. Seventy-two divided by 8 is 9. Nine times 3 is 27 and minus 2 is 25. Then I added 1 and got 26.

Many of the students are certain that their answer is correct, and when the teacher asks about the order of operations, all of the students refer to PEMDAS, as if that explains their reasons for finding the answers that they did. She gives a calculator to three different students and asks them to find the answer. All report an answer of twenty-six. They start to review the answer in terms of PEMDAS when Eko says, "Wait, I forgot; it's like they're in pairs. When you get to the pair, you do it left to right. So we can divide first if it comes before multiplication."

The teacher tells the students that many people get confused about this and she thinks they should make a new saying to help them remember. She displays the text *the perfect eggs or eggs that are perfect* and says, "This can remind us that we can do parentheses before exponents or exponents before parentheses." Then she asks students to think of a food that begins with *d*. When they finish, they have a sign that reads:

PE/MD/AS
the perfect eggs or eggs are perfect
the magnificent dumplings or dumplings are magnificent
the awesome soup or soup is awesome

She knows most students won't remember this entire list of phrases, but she believes that its creation will help them remember how to apply PEMDAS correctly. (Later in the day, while walking to lunch, she enjoys overhearing a student ask, in an excellent British accent, "I say, do you think we'll have magnificent dumplings or dumplings that are magnificent today?")

She introduces the game and asks a volunteer to roll the dice. She has the students work in teams of four to create the equations, all using the numbers shown on the dice. The class reviews a variety of the equations and checks them for accuracy, and then teams are ready to play their own games.

Tips from the Classroom

❯ When we field-tested this game, students told us that they thought two minutes was just the right amount of time, but you should adjust the time if you find it is not right for your students.

❯ Though having a calculator is optional, we found that it was helpful for students to check when they disagreed about the accuracy of an equation and to identify misconceptions.

⟩ It is likely that your students will work cooperatively in different ways. We found some teams did everything together; some teams assigned different decades to each player; and some worked alone first, shared their thinking, and then worked together to find values they still needed.

⟩ Some students wanted to record all of the equations they found within each decade. We found that approach often kept them stuck in one or two decades, but we did create a variation that met students' wish to do this. (See "Variations.")

⟩ Because teams are working with the same numbers, you may wish to have them work behind an upright file folder to preserve the privacy of their choices.

What to Look For

⟩ Do players' equations vary, or do they seem to get stuck in a pattern, relying on only one or two operations, only two numbers, or only one-digit numbers?

⟩ What examples of relational thinking are noted that you want to share with other students?

⟩ How do students communicate the order of operations? Do they use words, write several equations, or add appropriate parentheses as needed?

⟩ What happens when opponents disagree on the accuracy of an equation?

Variations

⟩ Allow for decimal points to be added to the numbers rolled.

⟩ Require players to use different operations in their equations; for example, students cannot use only addition in all of their equations.

⟩ Use a three-minute timer and allow players who have found one equation for each decade to record all the different equations they find for the decades, as long as their values are different. Players can receive a point for each one.

Exit Card Choices

⟩ If you rolled 2, 4, 5, and 6, what are two expressions you could create equal to a number in the seventies? (Possibilities include $62 + 5 + 4 = 71$; $6 \times 5 + 42 = 72$; $4 \times 2 + 65 = 73$; and $64 + 5 \times 2 = 74$.)

⟩ A student wrote the equation $36 \div 6 \times 2 + 3 = 15$. Her partner said that the equation was not true and that it should be equal to 6. What do you think and why?

Extension

Create a space where students can add their own creative transformations of *Please pity my dear Aunt Sally* or *PEMDAS* to pairs of phrases that reinforce the appropriate interpretation of the rule.

Calculator Target

Why This Game or Puzzle?

We often perform multidigit computation on calculators, and it is important that we know how to estimate the results to make sure we have entered the information correctly. We may use front-end estimation, rounding, or compatible numbers to make an estimate, often the only computation required in real-world situations. Unfortunately, students are less able to estimate than to calculate exact values (Van de Walle, Karp, and Bay-Williams 2013).

In this game, once an outcome or target is identified by turning over three cards, each team chooses an operation and a number for the opposing team to work with. Both teams then privately choose another number and enter their expressions into their calculators to find the total value. They see how close their answers are to the target number, with the scoring advantage given to the team with the closer value. Although the game is described with whole numbers, a decimal card is provided for those who wish to include it in the game.

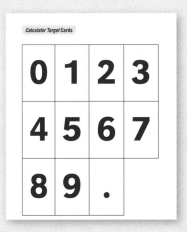

Calculator Target Cards

0	1	2	3
4	5	6	7
8	9	.	

Math Focus

› Estimating sums, differences, products, and quotients
› Computing differences

Materials Needed

› 1 calculator per team
› 1 deck of *Calculator Target* Cards per group (decimal point card is optional) (page A-59)
› 1 *Calculator Target* Recording Sheet per team (page A-60)
› 1 *Calculator Target* Directions per group (page A-61)

Directions

Goal: Complete expressions to meet or get close to the target numbers.
› Shuffle the deck of *Calculator Target* cards and place them facedown.

> Team 1 turns over the top three cards of the deck and uses the numbers to form a three-digit number. This number is the target number for round 1, and both teams should write it on their recording sheets.

> Teams exchange recording sheets, and opposing teams record an operation sign in the square for round 1 and a number that is less than the target number in the blank immediately to the right of that sign.

> Teams return recording sheets, and without using paper and pencil or a calculator, each team quickly writes a number in the blank to the left of the operation sign.

> Teams then use their calculators to complete the equations.

> Each team determines its points for this round by finding the difference between its answer and the target number, subtracting from the greater number. Each team records its points for this round.

> Reshuffle the cards. Team 2 turns three cards over and forms the target number for round 2, and teams once again exchange recording sheets.

> Teams continue to alternate forming the three-digit numbers for five rounds. Then teams find their total points. The team with the fewer number of points wins.

How It Looks in the Classroom

One fifth-grade teacher has noticed that her students always use the rounding strategy for making estimates. For example, when asked to estimate $476 \div 7$, many of them are more likely to transform the expression to $480 \div 7$ than to $490 \div 7$. She has decided that this game will provide a good opportunity to review the compatible-number estimation strategy for division. She also wants students to practice using it at the same time in which other strategies are likely to be used for the other operations. She begins the lesson by displaying the expression $724 + 168$ and asking students to talk at their tables about the strategies they could use to estimate the sum. She writes *We _____ to estimate a sum of _____* to help students prepare their responses.

When the teacher asks for responses, Marcus shares his completed sentence as, "*We added* 700 *and* 200 *to estimate a sum of* 900."

Olga says, "We started like Marcus by rounding to 700, but then it was easy to just add 178 to estimate a sum of 878."

Elisabeth says, "We just looked at the first digits to estimate a sum of 800."

Then the teacher displays $336 \div 4$ and the frame *We _____ to estimate a quotient of _____* and again asks them to talk at their tables. She immediately notices that there isn't as much conversation. This time Jesse shares first by saying, "We thought about 340 divided by 4, but then we didn't know what to do."

Will says, "We started to divide and found that thirty-three divided by four was about eight to estimate a quotient of eighty."

Jenna asks, "How did you get eighty?" The teacher asks someone else from Will's group to respond.

Lucinda explains, "It's not just thirty-three divided by four; it's thirty-three tens, so the answer has to be in tens, too. Do you get that?"

Jenna shakes her head to indicate that she doesn't, so Lucinda adds, "You can't just forget about the six. You have to have a number about that, too. We're estimating, so we just put a zero there."

Pablo adds, "I think it would help to think about 320 divided by 4, because that is really what we were doing."

The teacher wants to build on what Pablo just said. She writes *271 ÷ 4* on chart paper and underneath it she writes *300 ÷ 4, 270 ÷ 4,* and *280 ÷ 4.* She asks, "Which example would help you the most?" Once they agree on the last one, she asks them to create an example for 538 ÷ 6 with numbers that are helpful, or compatible.

Following this introduction, she tells students they are going to play a game involving estimation and they should think about the different strategies they use. She plays two rounds with the whole class and then students play in teams.

Tips from the Classroom

❯ We found that most students were comfortable with making quick estimates as long as they could use their calculators to find exact answers. However, if some players are taking too long, you could include a timer.

❯ Students told us that they enjoyed making difficult problems for their opponents. Be sure to look at recording sheets to learn what students identified as challenging.

❯ If you have ten-sided dice available that show the numbers 0 through 9, students could use those rather than the cards; it is easier to roll three dice than to reshuffle and turn over three cards for each round.

What to Look For

❯ Are students' estimates reasonable? Are estimates for some operations more reasonable than others?

❯ What estimation techniques do students use?

Variations

❯ Players could be required to use each of the four operations signs at least once.

❯ You could have students turn over four or more cards to form greater multidigit target numbers or only two cards to form smaller numbers.

❯ For extra challenge, include the decimal point card, which should be added to each target number to create a number with either tenths or hundredths.(For example, if students turned over 3, 6, and 4, they could decide to create the number 3.64 or 36.4.)

❯ Have one team identify the operation and the other team provide the number to the right of the sign, and then have both teams use this same information on their recording sheets.

Exit Card Choices

❯ How would you estimate 651 ÷ 8?

❯ The target number is 249. The opposing team wrote a multiplication sign and a *3* to the right of the sign. What number will you write to the left of the sign? How did you decide on that number without using paper and pencil or a calculator?

Extension

An elevator speech is a short speech that could be completed in about thirty seconds, or the time it takes to ride an elevator. Invite each student to write an elevator speech to give to a teacher titled "Why Your Students Should Play This Game."

Contig

Why This Game or Puzzle?

We found that the classic game *Contig* (Broadbent 1972) is still highly recommended by teachers, all these years later. In this game, players roll three dice and try to use the numbers shown to create an expression equal to an available number on the game board. As well as providing considerable practice with mental arithmetic, by encouraging students to brainstorm several unique responses in a short amount of time, the game increases both flexibility and fluency, two of the four aspects of creativity originally identified by Paul Torrance (1974) and still studied today.

One of the interesting features of the game is that players receive 1 point for each number on the board that their number touches. We've also added the rules that if opponents can create an expression and the team whose turn it is cannot, the opposing team receives those points, or if opponents can create an expression worth more points than the playing team did, the opponents receive the additional points. Together, these rules give players on *both* teams incentive to test several alternative combinations, no matter whose turn it is.

Math Focus

> Finding sums, differences, products, and quotients
> Using mental calculation
> Creating expressions for a given value

Contig Game Board							
1	2	3	4	5	6	7	8
9	10	11	12	13	14	15	16
17	18	19	20	21	22	23	24
25	26	27	28	29	30	31	32
33	34	35	36	37	38	39	40
41	42	44	45	48	50	54	55
60	64	66	72	75	80	90	96
100	108	120	125	144	150	180	216

Materials Needed

> 3 dice per group of players
> 1 *Contig* Game Board per group (page A-62)
> 1 *Contig* Recording Sheet per team (page A-63)
> Optional: 1 *Contig* Directions per group (page A-64)

Directions

Goal: Use numbers rolled on three dice to write expressions equal to numbers on the game board, getting points for those numbers and any numbers they touch.

> Each team selects a player to roll a die. The team with the lesser number plays first.
> Take turns.
> On each turn you roll three dice and use each of the numbers exactly once, along with any of the four operations, to write an expression. You can use more than one operation or use the same operation twice.
> Simplify your expression and confirm the accuracy with your opponent.
> Look for the answer on the *Contig* Game Board and if it is not already marked, mark it with an X. This number may not be marked again. Write your equation on the *Contig* Recording Sheet.
> You get 1 point for creating an expression equal to an unmarked number on the board and 1 point for each other *marked* number next to it (in a row, column, or diagonal).
> If the opposing team can create an expression with the same numbers that's worth more points, it gets the additional points. If you can't find a solution on your turn, and the other team can, that team gets all those points. In either case, the opposing team's number is not marked.

> So in the mini-board shown below, if you could mark 29, you would receive 2 points: 1 point for 29 and 1 for 21, as it touches 29. If your opposing team could find an expression equal to 20, it would be worth 3 points: 1 for the 20, 1 for touching the 13, and 1 for touching the 21. You would still get your 2 points, but the opposing team would get 1 point because those players found an expression that resulted in a total number of points worth 1 more point than yours.

11	12	13̶
19	20	2̶1̶
27	28	29

> If you are unable to get a number that is unmarked, you score 0 points for the turn. If your opposing team can, that team receives the number of points that its number is worth.
> Play a total of six rounds. The team with the greater total score is the winner.

How It Looks in the Classroom

One fourth-grade teacher begins by rolling three dice on a piece of paper placed under her projection device. The dice show the values 2, 4, and 6. She tells students they will have two minutes to use these three numbers to write expressions with different values. On the paper she writes:

> You must use each number exactly once in each expression.
> Each expression must have a different value.
> You can use two different operations or the same one twice.

She says, "Ready, begin." After an appropriate amount of time, students share some of their equations, which the teacher records for all to see and to check for accuracy. Then the teacher displays the game board and says, "In this game you roll three dice and use the numbers, just like we did, to match a number on the game board."

The teacher rolls the three dice and says, "The students on the right will be one team. Create an expression using the numbers rolled." The team creates an expression equal to twelve. The teacher crosses out that number on the board and tells the students, "Once a number is used, we cross it out to show that it can't be used again. The team gets 1 point."

The teacher rolls the dice again, turns to the students on the left side and says, "Now it is your turn. You will get 1 point for an expression with a value on the board other than twelve. You will also get a point if your number touches the 12." Then turning to the opposing team, she says, "You should look, too. If they can't find an expression equal to a number that touches the 12 and you do, you'll get the extra point."

After two more rounds, students play the game in their own teams.

Tips from the Classroom

〉 Having players think aloud as they brainstorm expressions is helpful, as it allows partners to build on each other's thinking.

〉 Sometimes moving a die next to another one triggers a new idea. You may want to model this strategy for students.

〉 Some players will use only the top part of the board because they prefer working with those numbers. For some, this may be an appropriate choice; others may need to be encouraged to try a different part of the board.

What to Look For

〉 Are students computing and recording their thinking accurately?

〉 When limited to the use of just three numbers, what strategies do students use to brainstorm expressions with different values?

〉 When it's not their turn, are opponents also trying to find expressions for extra points?

〉 Do students show a preference for particular numbers or operations?

Variations

〉 You can condense the game board by eliminating the last one or two rows or, for more challenge, the top two rows.

〉 The game can be played without the scoring system but, rather, to get three or four in a row, column, or diagonal.

〉 Students can use thirty-second or one-minute timers if you prefer to keep the game short in duration.

Exit Card Choices

〉 All of the numbers 1–42 are shown on the game board, but not all of the numbers 43–216. Why do you think specific numbers are missing?

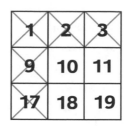

> Your game board is above. On your turn, you roll 2, 5, and 2. What is your best move, and how many points would you get?

> How would you correct this equation: $2 + 6 \times 3 = 24$?

Extension

There is a classic puzzle called *Four 4s* that requires solvers to write equations, each using exactly four 4s and any operations needed, for instance, $(4 + \frac{4}{4}) \times 4 = 20$. The goal is to find equations for the values 0 through 100. Your students can try a miniature version of this puzzle, with the goal of finding equations for the values 0 through 9.

Most online games and apps for mixed operations focus on having players solve enough equations correctly so they can shoot at a target or complete a picture

Online Games and Apps

as a reward. A few alternatives to such practice require students to use relational thinking, to practice the order of operations to reach a target number, or to practice with all operations within one game. Playing online games may be beneficial to students who are making a good deal of errors, as the online environment often allows for students to see their errors instantly. Also, online games involving logic or problem solving are often of more interest to students than those games that merely show a computation example and flash "Good job" when the player completes it correctly. Here are a few examples:

• Crackers and Goo (http://www.crackersandgoo.com/) is an app in which students practice addition and multiplication, with the goal of identifying and extending color and number patterns made of crackers. Once a pattern is complete, students must calculate the total value of the crackers in the last pattern. The total may be computed by recognizing the numerical pattern from previous figures in the pattern or by looking for a pattern within the last figure.

For example, students are given a geometric pattern in which they observe an increasing number of 198s. The last figure in the pattern must be totaled by multiplying to find 5×198 or using repeated addition. Students are given the opportunity to use repeated addition or to learn the round-and-multiply strategy, solving the equation $5 \times 200 - 5 \times 2 = x$. With a number of difficulty levels, students are provided with a visual approach to practicing such skills as repeated addition leading to multiplication, rounding, and estimation.

- Order Ops is a free game found on Mr. Nussbaum's website at http://www.mrnussbaum.com/orderops/ in which the player must solve problems involving order of operations to advance up a set of stairs to save members of a royal family from demise. The unique features of this game involve allowing students to choose which part of an expression to solve first, using the correct order of operations. Many other games of this sort then simply tell the user the correct answer and continue on, but this game requires students to choose one part of the expression and simplify it themselves. If they are correct, the program then replaces the students' answer into the expression and continues as such until the value of the expression is found. Students are able to fully visualize each step of the problem while being actively involved in solving it.

- The $+\times/-$ Mahjong Games, free games found on the Sheppard Software website at http://www.sheppardsoftware.com/mathgames/mixed_mahjong/mahjongMath_Level_1.html, are played on a Mahjong-style game board with tiles labeled either with expressions or with one- or two-digit numbers. Students must match the tiles in order to remove them from the game board, attempting to clear the entire board in order to win. Tiles may be removed by matching an expression with its numerical value or another expression with the same value, encouraging the player to use relational thinking. For example, any two of the following tiles could be matched: 8×3, 6×4, $20 + 4$, and 24. As an added challenge, tiles may not be removed unless they are not "blocked in" by other tiles, thereby creating a need to choose tiles strategically.

Fractions

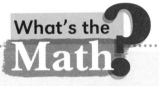

You only have to see young children share an apple or a cookie to know that they have a great deal of intuitive knowledge of fractions. They may also have or develop misconceptions or partial understandings related to fractions. For instance, children may think that you get halves by dividing something into two parts, without concern for the equivalence of those parts. Students may learn that a fraction is merely the number of shaded parts "over" or "out of" the total number of parts. Not only is this model inadequate, but it makes no sense when applied to fractions such as seven-sixths. How can seven of six parts be shaded? Perhaps as a result of such issues, it is reported that students and teachers find working with fractions to be challenging (Lamon 2012). Games and puzzles in this chapter build on students' conceptual ideas while addressing their misunderstandings.

Visual images of *iterating* (copying or repeating) parts and *partitioning* wholes help students better understand the relationships between a fraction's numerator and denominator (Siebert and Gaskin 2006). A part can be iterated to form a whole. For example, a unit fraction of one-fourth can be iterated four times to make one whole. A whole of one can be partitioned into three equal pieces, with each identified as one-third. Figure 7.1 illustrates these examples. Note that when you apply such thinking to fractions with a numerator greater than its denominator, seven-sixths is seven one-sixths, avoiding the notion of seven "out of" six.

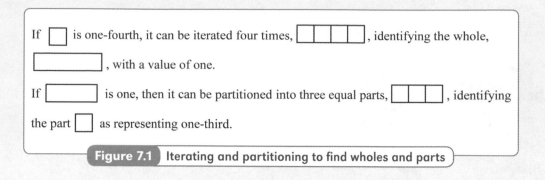

If ▢ is one-fourth, it can be iterated four times, ▢▢▢▢ , identifying the whole, ▢▢▢▢▢ , with a value of one.

If ▢▢▢ is one, then it can be partitioned into three equal parts, ▢▢▢ , identifying the part ▢ as representing one-third.

Figure 7.1 Iterating and partitioning to find wholes and parts

The iterating and partitioning processes can also be applied to the number line, by using a one-dimensional, rather than two-dimensional, model. Understanding fractions on number lines is complex (Psycharis, Latsi, and Kynigos 2009), and we need to help students think about fractions on a number line in the same way as they do whole numbers, that is, points that represent distances from 0. Students must also view a fraction as one number, not two, to avoid misconceptions related to whole number thinking. For example, students might conclude that ⅝ is greater than ¾, as 5 is greater than 3 and 8 is greater than 4.

The importance of emphasizing that fractions are numbers cannot be overstated. Many, if not most, students think fractions are a separate category. As such, they do not tend to recognize that some strategies used for whole number computation also apply to fractions. For example, students know from a very early age that whole numbers can be decomposed and composed, yet it does not occur to most children or adults that they can find + ⅓ by thinking + ⅙ + ⅙. With so many potential partial understandings, it is vital that students have many opportunities to explore concepts and practice skills.

Unit Fractions and Wholes

Why This Game or Puzzle?

Clarke, Roche, and Mitchell (2008) recommend that we provide a variety of models to represent fractions. Cuisenaire Rods (see Figure 7.2) allow relationships among parts and wholes to be investigated within a length model. If these rods are not available, you can use the similar two-dimensional models provided on page A-65.

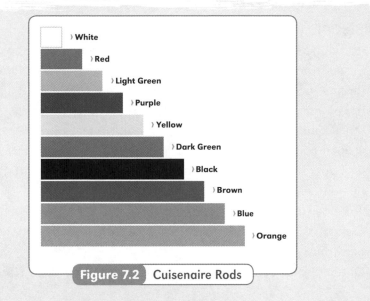

Figure 7.2 Cuisenaire Rods

In this game, players assign a value of either a unit fraction (a fraction with a numerator of one) or a whole (one) to one of their rods and then ask questions such as *If this rod* [showing rod] *is one whole, do you have one-fourth?* and *If this rod is one-fifth, do you have one whole?* The many relationships between unit fractions and wholes that the rods can model are shown in Figure 7.3.

Whole	Unit Fractions
Red	White is ½.
Light Green	White is ⅓.
Purple	White is ¼; Red is ½.
Yellow	White is ⅕.
Dark Green	White is ⅙; Red is ⅓; Light Green is ½.
Black	White is ⅐.
Brown	White is ⅛; Red is ¼; Purple is ½.
Blue	White is ⅑; Light Green is ⅓; Dark Green is ⅔.
Orange	White is ¹/₁₀; Red is ⅕; Yellow is ½.

Figure 7.3 Relationships between unit fractions and wholes modeled with rods

Math Focus

› Understanding relationships between a unit fraction and one whole
› Identifying unit fractions and wholes
› Creating a unit fraction, given one whole, or creating one whole, given a unit fraction

Materials Needed

› 1 opaque bag containing the following Cuisenaire Rods or 1 set of pieces from the top part of *Unit Fractions and Wholes* Rod Models (page A-65) per group of players: 9 white (W), 5 red (R), 3 light green (LG), 2 purple (P), 2 yellow (Y), 3 dark green (DG), 1 black (K), 3 brown (N), 3 blue (E), and 3 orange (O)

› 1 open collection of Cuisenaire Rods or 1 set of pieces from the bottom part of *Unit Fractions and Wholes* Rod Models per group for students to use to check their thinking (page A-65)

› 1 die per group

› Optional: 1 set of *Unit Fractions and Wholes* Rod Colors and Letters per group (page A-66)

› Optional: 1 *Unit Fractions and Wholes* Directions per group (page A-67)

Directions

Goal: To collect the greater number of pairs of rods.

› Shake the bag of rods to mix them up. Place the bag and open collection of rods in the center of the play area.

› Without looking, each team draws six rods from the bag, one at a time, taking turns. Put the chosen rods in your laps, out of view of the opposing team.

› A member of each team rolls a die and the greater number indicates the team that plays first.

› On each turn, the team chooses one of its rods and decides to identify it as one whole or a unit fraction. Then it asks the opposing team if it has either a certain unit fraction or a whole. For example, if Team 1 chooses a purple rod, and decides that rod will represent one whole, one of the players might say, "This purple rod is one whole. Do you have one-half?"

  › If Team 2 has a red rod, one of its players can say, "Yes, here is the red, which is one-half of the purple." Teams can use the open collection of rods to show this relationship. Team 1 has made a pair and puts the purple and red rods in its pile. Then each team chooses one replacement rod from the bag without looking.

  › If Team 2 does not have a red rod, a member can reply, "No, we don't have a red, which would be one-half of the purple." Team 1 must draw another rod from the bag, and its turn has ended.

  › Note that Team 1 could have chosen the purple rod and said, "This purple rod is one-half. Do you have one whole?" In this case, the other team would check to see if it had a brown rod and show that, since it takes two purples to make a brown, brown would be one whole.

› The game ends when one of the teams no longer has any rods, or there are no more rods in the bag and no matches to be made with the rods the players have left. The winner is the team with the greatest number of pairs.

How It Looks in the Classroom

(Note: If your students are using the two-dimensional rods in the appendix, display or distribute copies of *Unit Fractions and Wholes* Rod Colors and Letters. Ask students to explain why the particular letters were chosen as identifiers. [First letters are used except with colors that all begin with *b*. In this case, last letters are used.] Leave this code available as long as necessary, but use and encourage students to use the actual color names.)

One third-grade teacher provides open collections of rods to each group of four students and gives a few minutes for them to refamiliarize themselves with the manipulatives. She then rings the classroom chime to bring their attention back to her, places a dark green rod on the projection device, and says, "I am going to ask you a question. Use the rods to help you answer. If this dark green rod represents one whole, what do you think would represent one-half?"

She gives students time to consider the task and then invites them to talk with their neighbors about which rod they chose and to make another choice if they change their minds. She displays the following sentence frame and asks students to use it to tell how they know their choice is correct: *If _____ is one whole, then _____ is _____ because_____.*

As a class they decide that light green is one-half of dark green, because if they split the dark green into two equal parts, one part would be the same length as the light green. (Students may also recognize that it takes two light greens to make one dark green.) The teacher then shows the orange rod and says, "If this rod is one whole, what is one-fifth?" Again, she asks students to complete the sentence frame when they state the answer (red).

Next the teacher poses a different kind of question. She asks, "If white is one-fourth, what is one whole?" She encourages students to use the rods to check their thinking. This time she draws students' attention to this sentence frame: *If _____ is _____, then we know that _____ is one whole because _____.* The class agrees with one student's statement: "If the white rod is one-fourth, then the purple is one whole because it takes four whites to make a length as long as the purple."

The teacher asks another question: "If this red rod is one-fourth, then what is one whole?"

After these examples the teacher demonstrates several rounds of the game, using two prepared bags of rods. She empties the rods from the class bag and projects them for all to see. She shows a red rod and asks, "If red is one whole, do you have one-half?" After a few turns, with volunteers responding and then choosing a rod from the class set and posing a question, she gives each group of four students the opaque bags of rods and open collections, and they play their own games.

Tips from the Classroom

❭ You may wish to use actual rods, rather than paper models, even if this means the game can be explored by only one small group at a time because the rods provide a stronger tactile experience.

❭ If the rods are new to students, be sure to give adequate time for them to become familiar with the manipulatives, as it will improve their success with the game.

❭ Some students find it helpful to have one example of each rod, placed one next to the other, in a staircase progression, or a pictorial model of the staircase on a laminated card.

❭ Some students requested graph paper and colored pencils so that they could record their moves.

❭ Some students prefer to place rods end-to-end to test a conjecture, while others would rather "stamp" a shorter rod across the top of a longer one. As long as they can do so accurately, either method is fine.

What to Look For

❭ Do students use the extra rods to check their thinking?

❭ What evidence do you see that students are using iterative and partitive thinking?

❭ What relationships between the rods are students recognizing automatically?

❭ Do some students seem to prefer questions that begin with unit fractions or with the whole?

❭ What language do students use to describe their thinking?

❭ Do students develop any strategies for choosing rods from the bag?

Variations

❭ Have students play the game with both teams' rods visible.

❭ Have students play cooperatively, with opponents providing one piece of information, for instance, "We have a yellow rod," before the other team poses its question.

❭ Include non-unit fractions, allowing questions such as "If this rod is two-thirds, do you have one whole?"

❭ You may wish to provide students with the two sentence stems referred to earlier and require students to complete one of the sentences whenever a pair is formed:

If _____ is one whole, then we know that _____ is _____ because _____.

If _____ is _____, then we know that _____ is one whole because _____.

Exit Card Choices

〉 If you know the rod that is one whole, how can you check to see if another rod is one-fifth?

〉 If you know the rod that is one-third, how can you identify the rod that is one whole?

〉 Apply your thinking to the number line. Where does 1 belong? How do you know?

$\frac{1}{4}$

Extension

〉 Offer a visual challenge involving partitioning and iterating. For example: *If* ☐ *represents ⅜, draw a rectangle to show 1⅝ .*

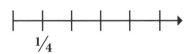

Name That Number

Why This Game or Puzzle?

Communicating mathematical ideas and sharing mathematical thinking are essential habits of mind. For this puzzle, team members must share what they know in order to have all of the necessary data to find the solution. The need to collect data is relevant to almost all real-world problem-solving situations, as is the need to cooperate. Cooperation and communication were identified as two of the four skills now needed for learning and innovation by the Partnership for 21st Century Skills (2008).

Here, a logic number puzzle is solved cooperatively, based on a model for cooperative problem solving suggested by Tim Erickson (1989). Each member of a three-person, cooperative team is given two clues about a fraction. The players must decide how to share and organize the information as they try to identify the fraction that meets all of the clues. We chose to call the puzzle *Name That Number* rather than *Name That Fraction* to remind students that fractions are numbers. Three levels of the puzzle are provided (pages A-68–A-70). It is likely that the first puzzle is most appropriate for third graders, the second one for fourth graders, and the third one for fifth graders, though you may find at least two of the puzzles at the right level for some of your students.

Math Focus

› Comparing fractions
› Adding and subtracting fractions with common denominators
› Multiplying fractions and whole numbers

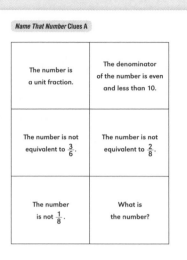

Name That Number **Clues A**

The number is a unit fraction.	The denominator of the number is even and less than 10.
The number is not equivalent to $\frac{3}{6}$.	The number is not equivalent to $\frac{2}{8}$.
The number is not $\frac{1}{8}$.	What is the number?

Materials Needed

› 1 set of *Name That Number* Clues A, B, or C per team of three students (page A-68, A-69, or A-70)
› Optional: 1 *Name That Number* Directions per team (page A-71)

Directions

Goal: Use the clues to find the mystery fraction.

› Form a team of three puzzle solvers.
› Place the clues facedown. Each solver randomly takes two of the clues.
› Solvers may read their clues to the others, but may not show the clues.
› Work together to figure out the number being described by the clues. Read the clues as many times as necessary, and talk about what you know.
› You can write or draw to help you understand the information in the clues, but you can't record the clues.
› When you think you have the solution, read the clues again to check.

How It Looks in the Classroom

A fourth-grade teacher introduces the puzzle with a simpler version involving whole numbers, so that she can emphasize how to solve the puzzle before thinking about the fractions puzzle. She has created the six clues shown in Figure 7.4. She calls students to bring their pencils and math journals to the morning meeting area. Then she invites three volunteers to sit in the middle of the circle. She tells them that the three students in the center circle will be the solvers and those in the larger circle will be the careful observers. She tells the observers that they can write any notes they wish as the students in the center circle try to solve the puzzle and observe the communication in the group. She places the six clues facedown inside the solvers' circle and tells the three students to each choose two of the clues, but not to show them.

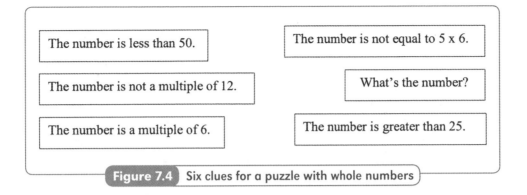

The number is less than 50.

The number is not equal to 5 x 6.

The number is not a multiple of 12.

What's the number?

The number is a multiple of 6.

The number is greater than 25.

Figure 7.4 Six clues for a puzzle with whole numbers

The teacher directs the solvers to read the clues aloud one at a time, in any order they choose, and to talk about what they learn from each clue. She also lets them know that clues may be read again, after all other clues have been heard, and that they may make lists of numbers, but not record the clues.

Henry begins and reads, "The number is not equal to five times six."

Jasmine follows up with "So it's not thirty. My first clue says, 'The number is less than fifty.'"

The students continue reading the clues one by one, but no one writes anything down yet. Then Misha suggests, "Let's review what we know, like what it is between." The group agrees and reads the two relevant clues again. Jasmine and Henry debate about whether to write all of the numbers between twenty-five and fifty or review another clue. While they are talking, Misha writes these numbers and, when finished, says, "Look, I have them. Let's read the clues and cross off the numbers that don't work." They agree to do so and soon find the solution, forty-two.

The teacher models the checking process by asking the solvers to reread the clues, one at a time, and confirm that their number matches each of them. Then she asks the observers and the solvers to discuss communication and strategies. She asks for compliments first and students agree that the solvers followed directions, only one person spoke at a time, and making a list was helpful. Then the teacher asks, "What could be done better as you work together?"

Fisher says, "I think it helped that Misha made the list, but maybe she should have talked to Jasmine and Henry about it first."

Lisa says, "Maybe Henry and Jasmine could have asked her what she was doing." It is decided that groups of solvers should pay attention to each other and work together.

The teacher explains that they will now all solve a similar puzzle using numbers that are fractions. She encourages them to follow the directions as Jasmine, Henry, and Misha did, and to discuss their own strategies and communication after they reach a solution.

Tips from the Classroom

❯ Most students are likely to want paper and pencil for listing possible numbers and then crossing off candidates as they are eliminated through the clues.

❯ Through field testing of this puzzle we discovered some students wanted to show each other the cards despite the requirement to only read the clues aloud. Teachers may want to reinforce the goal of having students listen to each other.

❯ It may be helpful for some students to have a fraction manipulative or chart available to them such as the one shown in Figure 7.5.

❯ We found that several groups wanted to create their own sets of clues to exchange with another group.

1											
1/2						1/2					
1/3				1/3				1/3			
1/4			1/4			1/4			1/4		
1/5		1/5		1/5		1/5			1/5		
1/6		1/6		1/6		1/6		1/6		1/6	
1/8	1/8	1/8	1/8	1/8	1/8	1/8	1/8				
1/10	1/10	1/10	1/10	1/10	1/10	1/10	1/10	1/10	1/10		
1/12	1/12	1/12	1/12	1/12	1/12	1/12	1/12	1/12	1/12	1/12	1/12

Figure 7.5 Fraction chart

What to Look For

❯ Do students rely on drawing, models, diagrams, written computation, mental computation, and/or recognition?

❯ What strategies do students use for organizing information?

❯ How do students work together? Do they make sure everyone participates? Do roles such as facilitator and note taker evolve as the students work on the puzzle?

Variations

❯ Have solvers show their clues one at a time, without talking or gesturing. After all the clues have been shown, each solver may rearrange the order of one of the clues. Through eye contact, rather than talking, solvers communicate that they think they have a solution. Solvers may then talk to check the clues.

❯ Solvers may choose a clue and write down all possible solutions given only that clue, using an ellipsis (…) to indicate the list does not have an ending yet. As each subsequent clue is revealed, the possible solutions may be eliminated until only one solution remains.

❯ If you choose to make your own *Name That Number* cards, you could increase or decrease the complexity level by adding a sixth clue and eliminating the card that states *What is the number?*

Exit Card Choices

❯ How might you represent the information you gain from the clue *It is between ¼ and ¾?*

❯ How did your team decide to share your clues?

❭ What was helpful about working together to solve the puzzle? What was challenging?

See Figure 7.6 for a student's response to the second exit card question.

Extension

Have students contribute a phrase or a picture to a poster titled "Cooperative Puzzle Solving."

> I READ THE FIRST CLUE AND THEN WE DECIDED WHAT THE POSSIBILITIES WERE. THEN, MY PARTNER CHOSE A SECOND CLUE TO READ THAT HE THOUGHT WOULD HELP US TO CROSS OUT SOME OF THE CHOICES. WE KEPT READING CLUES UNTIL WE GOT THE ANSWER, BUT IT WAS TRICKY SOMETIMES TO READ THE RIGHT CLUE SO WE HAD TO THINK ABOUT WHAT ~~WE~~ WOULD BE A GOOD CHOICE.

Figure 7.6 Student response to the second exit question

Order Up

Why This Game or Puzzle?

Comparing fractions requires conceptual understanding of the important relationship between the numerator and denominator; simply applying an algorithm does not support students' understanding of fractions or involve them in sense making. Depending on the particular fractions being compared, a variety of concepts can be applied. For example, when both numerators are the same, the fraction with the greater denominator is the number that is less because the size of the parts is smaller. As students often know equivalent names for one-half, comparisons to this benchmark number can also be helpful. Use of benchmark numbers is a key characteristic of number sense (Yang, Reys, and Wu 2010).

In this game, players are dealt five fractions cards, faceup, which they must keep in the order they were dealt. (See Figure 7.7.) On each turn they choose a card from the remaining cards, which are placed facedown in a seven-by-eight array, and may exchange it with any one of their cards or just return it to the array. The goal is to get the cards in their hands to be in order from least to greatest, left to right. The pace of a game situation encourages students to consider conceptual understanding, instead of always using an algorithmic approach. When such concepts cannot be applied to the random pairings of fractions in a game, students may use drawings, common denominators, or algorithms. Encourage students to use strategies flexibly and discourage them from always relying on an algorithm to compare fractions.

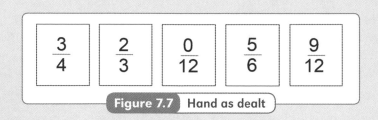

Figure 7.7 Hand as dealt

Math Focus

> Comparing numbers with a benchmark fraction
> Finding equivalent fractions
> Ordering fractions from least to greatest

Materials Needed

> 1 deck of *Order Up* Cards per group of players (made from *two* copies of pages A-72–A-74)
> Optional: 1 *Order Up* Directions per group (page A-75)

Directions

Goal: Exchange cards until the five numbers shown in your hand are in order from least to greatest, left to right.

> Shuffle the cards and place five cards faceup, from left to right, in front of each team. Teams may not change the order of the cards in their "hands." Put the remaining cards facedown in the middle of the play area in a seven-by-eight array, as you would in a concentration game.

> Decide who goes first. In this game, there is also an advantage to playing second because you will have seen one of the cards placed facedown in the array.

> You cannot rearrange your cards, but you will be able to exchange your cards for others that may work better in your hand. Note that two cards with equivalent values are not allowed. For example, if you have cards for ¾ and ⁶⁄₈, you cannot keep both of them, as they have the same value.

> The first team chooses any card from the array and may exchange this card with one of its five cards. If the team chooses to keep the card it has drawn, it puts the card it has removed from its hand face-down in the array to replace the taken card. If no exchange is made, the team puts the drawn card back in its location in the array.

> Teams take turns picking a card from the board and deciding whether or not to exchange it with a card in their hands.

> The first team to get its five fractions in order from least to greatest is the winner.

How It Looks in the Classroom

One fourth-grade teacher introduces this game by displaying two fractions: ⅚ and ⁵/₁₂. She asks students to compare these fractions and then talk with a partner about what they think. After a brief while, she asks the students to share their ideas. She lists a summary of what they say for all to see. Amir begins by saying, "Five-sixths is greater because you have five of each and the twelfths are smaller."

Zahra says, "I agree with Amir, but my reason is different. I think of each sixth as two-twelfths. That means five of them would be the same as ten-twelfths, and there are only five-twelfths in the other fraction."

Leila says, "I agree, but my reason is that five-sixths is greater than one-half and five-twelfths is less than one-half."

Kyle asks, "How do you know that?"

The conversation continues for a few more minutes and then the teacher introduces the game, explaining that this time the students will need to put five fraction cards in order. She deals two sets of five cards faceup under her projection device so all students can see them and arranges the remaining cards facedown on the table in a seven-by-eight array. She explains, "We want to order our cards from least to greatest," motioning from left to right, "but we can't just move them around. I am going to pick a card from the array of cards in front of me and see if I want to exchange it with one of my five cards." She draws a card and says, "I choose to replace my second card with this card, one-third, because five-sixths is too great a fraction for the second place in my hand. If I didn't want to trade, I'd have to put the card back and it would be your turn."

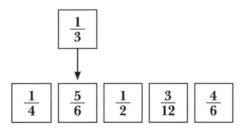

She then explains that the students, playing as a class, can now draw a card and see if they want to use it. She invites Evye to choose for the class. After a few more turns, the teacher has students summarize the rules of the game and then play in teams.

Tips from the Classroom

❯ Make a fraction chart (see Figure 7.5) available to some students to refer to when they are uncertain of the order or as a way for groups to check the winning order.

❯ Some students automatically look for common denominators; encourage them to consider other strategies as well.

❯ Have some students create their own sets of cards with visual models on them, such as number lines or parts of wholes, which players can use to help them compare the numbers.

What to Look For

❭ Do students recognize fractions equivalent to one-half and one whole?

❭ How do students use benchmark numbers?

❭ What evidence of misunderstandings do you observe?

❭ What models of fractions do students refer to or draw?

Variations

❭ Reduce the number of cards in each hand to four or increase it to six.

❭ Add fraction cards with denominators that are not factors of twelve, for example, fifths, eighths, and tenths.

❭ With a different set of cards, this same game could be played with (or include) mixed numbers or decimal numbers.

Exit Card Choices

❭ Should the card showing ¼ go to the left or the right of the card showing ⅓? Explain how you know.

❭ Choose five cards from the deck of *Order Up* Cards and place them so that each card is equivalent to or less than the card on its right. Write the numbers.

❭ One team thinks it has won, but its cards show ⅖ as greater than ¾. Write and draw to show the team that ¾ is greater than ⅖.

Extension

Give students the following writing assignment: *Write in your journal about different ways to decide which of two fractions is greater or if they are equivalent. Include why you should have a variety of strategies to compare fractions.*

Fraction Action

Why This Game or Puzzle?

As mentioned earlier in this chapter, whole number thinking can lead some students to order fractions incorrectly, by comparing both numerators and both denominators rather than the relationship between each numerator and its denominator. Research suggests that students maintain misconceptions (Cramer, Post, and delMas 2002), so they are not likely to change the ways in which they see relationships unless they are in a situation that causes them to question their original thinking. Students need opportunities to talk about how they compare fractions and challenge each other's thinking. It is critical that we establish learning communities that support such interactions.

Along with ordering fractions, forming them with a particular goal in mind draws students' attention to the relative sizes of fractions and, thus, the relative relationship between the numerator and the denominator. This game also provides practice with addition and subtraction of fractions, as players try to form expressions with two fractions to get the least (or greatest) values.

Math Focus

› Comparing fractions
› Adding and subtracting fractions

Materials Needed

› 1 *Fraction Action* Game Board per team (page A-76)
› 1 deck of *Fraction Action* Cards per group of players (made from *two* copies of page A-77)
› Optional: 1 *Fraction Action* Directions per group (page A-78)

Fraction Action **Game Board**

Name(s): _____ Date: _____

Decide whether teams will try to get the least or greatest sums and differences. You'll receive 1 point each time your sum or difference is the least (or greatest).

Directions

Goal: Place numerators and denominators in the spaces on the game board, making fractions that—when added or subtracted—form the least or greatest sums and differences.

› Play with two or more teams.
› Shuffle the cards and place them facedown in a pile.
› Decide if the greatest or least sums or differences will receive a point.
› Turn over the top card.
› Each team separately decides in which of the twenty squares on its board to write the number. Be sure to note that two discard squares are available as choices. Once you've written a number, you cannot change it. When everyone has placed the number, turn over the next card.
› Play continues until all twenty squares on the game board have been filled.
› Each team adds and subtracts to complete the equations.
› Compare each sum or difference. The team with the greatest (or least) sum or difference gets 1 point.
› Write your total score. The team with the greatest (or least) total wins.

How Does It Work?

"Game time!" This is always a welcome phrase in this fifth-grade teacher's classroom. This teacher chooses to introduce *Fraction Action* by displaying one part of the game board (see Figure 7.8) on his projection device.

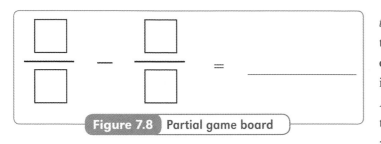

Figure 7.8 **Partial game board**

He holds one deck of the *Fraction Action* Cards in his hand and tells students that he will randomly ask someone to choose a card, which will then be placed in one of the empty squares in the display. After four cards have been placed, the teacher asks all students to compute the answer to the subtraction problem. He encourages students to share answers at their tables, confirming the correct answer before sharing with the class. Once all have agreed, the teacher then announces a new twist. He asks students to work together to see if a different arrangement of the numbers would create a difference that is greater.

As the teacher circulates, he hears Carla saying, "If we put the 3 in the numerator, it will make the second fraction smaller and that will make our difference bigger."

At another table, Seleem comments, "Let's put the 4 in the numerator and the 5 in the denominator of the first fraction because that's pretty close to one." The teacher appreciates the students' conversations about how moving the numbers will affect the final difference and is also pleased to see their understanding of how the relationship between the numerator and the denominator changes the size of the number.

Once students have rearranged the numbers and discussed the final results, the teacher tells the students they will now have the opportunity to turn this activity into a game. He reviews the directions of the game and hands out game boards and cards, encouraging them to use this same thinking about fraction relationships while playing the game.

Tips from the Classroom

❭ Some students may place numbers somewhat randomly at first and this is fine. They will learn from the outcomes of their initial examples.

❭ Some students will benefit from having a fraction manipulative available.

❭ Sometimes students forget that some of their whole number computation strategies can be applied to fractions. You may need to remind some students that they can, for example, "think addition" or use an open number line.

What to Look For

❭ What if-then thinking do students use as they discuss their choices?

❭ What evidence do you have that students recognize the relationship between the numerator and the denominator in a fraction?

❯ What strategies do students use to add and subtract?

❯ If students use drawings to help them subtract, do they use a take-away model or another meaning of subtraction, such as comparison?

Variations

❯ Choose particular target sums or differences for each equation and have each team's score be the difference between these targets and the actual sums and differences found. The lower score wins.

❯ Increase the number of cards in the deck and provide four discard boxes on the game board.

Exit Card Choices

❯ If you could use each of the numbers 1, 2, 3, and 4 only once and you wanted the greatest difference, where would you place them in this example?

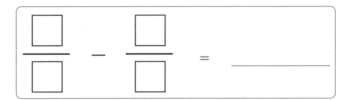

❯ Use an example from your game and explain how you compared the sums or differences to see which team received a point.

Figure 7.9 shows a response to the second exit question. Note that the student refers to the benchmark one-half.

I had 1 half and the other team had 11/24. The other team gets the point because 11/24 is less than one half. I know that 11/24 is less than one half because you would need another 24th to make it equal.

Figure 7.9 Sample student response to second exit card question

Extension

Students choose four of the cards, each showing a different number. Students then explore arrangements of the numerators and denominators to find how many different sums they can get.

Fraction Jigsaw

Why This Game or Puzzle?

The National Council of Teachers of Mathematics, in *Principles and Standards for School Mathematics* (NCTM 2000), identifies representations as essential to supporting students' understanding of mathematical concepts. For this puzzle students are given sixteen individual puzzle pieces that must be matched on all sides. Equivalent fractions with different representations make a match. To reach the solution they must decide how to sort and organize the information—decisions that are key in real-world situations.

Two versions of the puzzle are provided. The first puzzle requires students to match numerals, word names, and number lines with arrows identifying a particular fraction. The second version also includes computation with fractions and mixed numbers.

Math Focus

› Recognizing equivalent fractions
› Matching fractions with number line diagrams
› Matching fractions with denominators of tenths or hundredths to their decimal notations

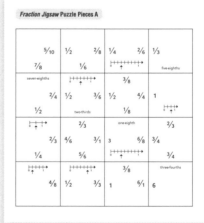

Materials Needed

› 1 set of *Fraction Jigsaw* Puzzle Pieces A or B per group of three to four students (page A-79 or A-80)
› Optional: 1 *Fraction Jigsaw* Directions per group (page A-81)

Directions

Goal: Arrange the puzzle pieces so that the numbers represented on all adjoining sides match.

› Work together.
› Organize all of the sixteen puzzle pieces into a square.
› The pieces should be placed so that the numbers on each of their sides match, that is, so that the numbers on the sides of any adjacent squares have the same value.
› Check to make sure you have matched each side correctly.

How It Looks in the Classroom

One fourth-grade teacher asks the class, "How could you represent four-eighths in different ways?"

As expected, one student suggests making a rectangle, dividing it into eight equal areas, and shading four of them. Irina talks about putting eight dimes in a piggy bank, four of which are shiny. José suggests, "You could write one-half or, really, any fraction that's the same as one-half." The teacher notes the absence of a number line and asks Benet to draw one on the board to show four-eighths.

The teacher compliments the students on their varied responses and then draws their attention to the board, where the teacher has displayed four cards similar to those in the puzzle. (See Figure 7.10, which also shows the solution.) The teacher asks Alihan to choose one side of one card, and he chooses the side with ¼. The teacher asks Alihan to call on another student to find a different representation for ¼, and Manny chooses ³⁄₁₂. The teacher asks yet another student to agree or disagree that the two representations are a match. When the students agree that they have found a match, the teacher moves these pieces together, placing the matching sides next to each other. Students continue to volunteer to complete the four-piece square.

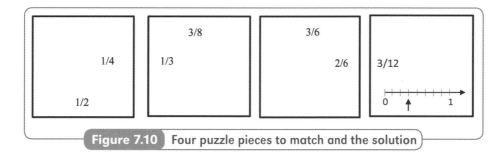

Figure 7.10 Four puzzle pieces to match and the solution

The teacher asks the students to describe the puzzle and they talk about matches on all sides. She then tells the class that each group will be given a set of cards similar to those displayed and students must match all the cards to form a square. The students are eager to begin.

Tips from the Classroom

〉 Students may have difficulty keeping the puzzle pieces in position once they find a match. Putting tape on the backs of the pieces keeps them stable, but moveable. Placing them on a piece of felt can also be helpful.

〉 Getting started is sometimes a challenge for students. Promote student conversation about where to begin and whether they want to split up the pieces to find matches or work together to match each piece. Try not to intercede in the conversation as they work through their strategies for solving the puzzle.

⟩ Encourage students who may need to visualize a fraction represented in another way than that in which it is presented to use a fraction manipulative or draw their own models on paper.

⟩ Some puzzle sides have more than one match. Students need to choose the piece that allows all sides to match. Some students did not notice this and thought there was an error in the puzzle when they were left with unmatched pieces. You may need to assure them that the puzzle works or, in some cases, ask them to see if there are pieces that could be exchanged.

What to Look For

⟩ Do some students have difficulty finding a particular type of representation to match another, such as number lines? If so, you may want to offer a small-group instructional opportunity.

⟩ Do students work together as a team to solve the puzzle, or do they try to work individually to match pieces?

⟩ Do students look for edges or corner pieces, transferring what they know about other jigsaw puzzles to this new situation? If so, encourage them to use this strategy in conjunction with what they know about the mathematics in the puzzle.

Variations

⟩ You can create less and more challenging examples of this puzzle by restricting or expanding the denominators, representations, and operations included.

⟩ Puzzle B (page A-80) can be made simpler by eliminating the bottom row, which includes multiplication of fractions. Cover this row and the bottom numbers in the row above it when making copies of the puzzle.

⟩ You can make the puzzle more challenging by putting numbers and representations on all sides of the puzzle pieces, requiring students to identify the pieces that have sides that do not have a match as the corners and edges.

Exit Card Choices

⟩ You are creating a fraction jigsaw puzzle. You want the solver to have to match $5/12$ with a number line diagram. Draw what you would show for the number line.

⟩ A friend has matched two puzzle pieces on one side but can't find two puzzle pieces to put above these pieces. He says, "This puzzle doesn't work." What might you say to your friend to be helpful?

Extension

Students can create their own miniature versions of this type of puzzle using the Make Your Own *Fraction Jigsaw* Puzzle Pieces Template (page A-82).

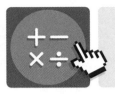

Online Games and Apps

Acquiring a conceptual understanding of the meaning of fractions involves a visual approach. There are numerous online games and apps requiring students to match a visual model of a fraction to its symbolic representation. Other online activities give students the opportunity to compute with fractions, often with the help of online manipulatives or pictorial representations of the problem. These visual models can deepen students' conceptual understanding as players explore naming, comparing and ordering, and computing with fractions. The online environment may provide some students with opportunities to manipulate these models in such a way as to more fully realize the concept than they would with a static model on paper. For others, working with concrete manipulatives is best.

Following are some examples:

- The Fraction Game, a free game found on NCTM's Illuminations website (go to http://illuminations.nctm.org/ and enter "fraction game" in the search box), shows students a series of number lines divided into different fractional amounts, each ending at 1. The goal is to move markers, which start at 0, to the end of the number lines using the fewest moves (cards) possible. For example, a player who draws the ⅗ card must move any number of spaces whose total value is less than or equal to ⅗ on a number line. A move of three spaces on the number line for fifths or six spaces on the number line for tenths would be appropriate. As a follow-up to this game, students may be asked to consider such questions as *What cards would be good to draw at the beginning of the game?* and *What would be the fewest number of moves possible to win the game?*

- The free app 4 Dice: A Fractions Game (http://www.mathfilefoldergames.com/my-math-apps/4-dice-fraction-games-app/) provides students with a target answer and an operation. The player then rolls four dice and chooses a placement for each die that will produce the correct answer. In the first levels of the game, players find equivalent fractions and order fractions. Players can move to tasks focusing on early addition and subtraction. Requiring conceptual thinking to find the targeted answer, the game often engages students in solving many different fraction problems prior to reaching the correct solution. Teachers may also track their students' progress and students may choose to challenge each other, providing extra motivation for moving through the levels.

- Fraction Feud, a free game found on the Calculation Nation website (go to http://calculationnation.nctm.org/ and click on "Play Games"), requires students to play against Calculation Nation or a human opponent chosen randomly to create a fraction that is more or less (depending upon the round of play) than their opponent's. Players choose two cards, one placed as the numerator, the other as the denominator. Each "joust," or round, will then proceed with two fewer cards than those available in the previous joust. At the end of each round, players have the opportunity to view why they won or lost the round. If students click on "Show me why I lost [or won]," the site displays a fraction bar chart, providing a visual representation of the two fractions. As well, students are provided with a written explanation to accompany the bar chart.

APPENDIX

Etiquette Expert Cards

Dear Etiquette Expert, Yesterday my good friend wanted to play a math game with me, but I knew it wouldn't help me learn. I didn't want to hurt her feelings, so I just played it. How could I have turned her down without hurting our friendship?	Dear Etiquette Expert, Whenever W.D. is on my team, he takes over. We are supposed to work together, but he never gives me a chance. He basically solves the puzzle all by himself. How can I keep him from doing this without looking like I am just whining?
Dear Etiquette Expert, Sometimes my partner gets really upset when we lose. She throws down the cards or dice and stomps off. Or sometimes she calls the other team names and says the game is boring. How can I help her to not be a sore loser?	Dear Etiquette Expert, I am a very shy person and get nervous when we have to form partners. I go sharpen a pencil or something. So usually I just end up with whoever is left. I don't even know how to get a partner. How can you help me?
Dear Etiquette Expert, My partner and I were working on a puzzle, but she just gave up. She said it was too hard and we shouldn't even bother to solve it. I thought we could solve it if we worked together. How can I convince her to work longer and that the effort is worth it?	Dear Etiquette Expert, My team doesn't clean up right. They just throw things in the box without sorting them. Sometimes important game pieces are left on the floor. I am getting tired of being the one to always put everything away correctly. What should I do?
Dear Etiquette Expert, Sometimes I really need to solve a puzzle alone. I get too distracted in the group and can't think about the math. I think my teacher might let me if I asked, but I'm worried about looking so different from everyone else. What do you think?	Dear Etiquette Expert, Yesterday my partner took a really long time. He had some good ideas, but it took forever for us to finish our turn because he wanted to check every possibility. How can we get the other team to be more patient and get my partner willing to stop?
Dear Etiquette Expert, The team we were playing against today made an error. I mentioned it and my partner said they should lose their turn. They got mad at me and said I wasn't the teacher and should just let it go. What do you suggest?	Dear Etiquette Expert, My team won today, but I was embarrassed by the big deal my partner made when we scored the final point. He kept telling the other team that we were much better than they were. What can I do if this happens again?
Dear Etiquette Expert, I'm not sure how to disagree with my partner when I think she is wrong, so sometimes I just agree with her. I don't want her to think I don't like her, but I want to talk more about our different ideas. What should I do?	Dear Etiquette Expert, My partner and I had a lot of questions about the puzzle today. We read the directions again, but it didn't help and everyone else looked busy. We finally just filled in some numbers and said we were done. What do you think we should have done instead?

Which Number Is Closest? Game Board

Name(s): _____   Date: _____

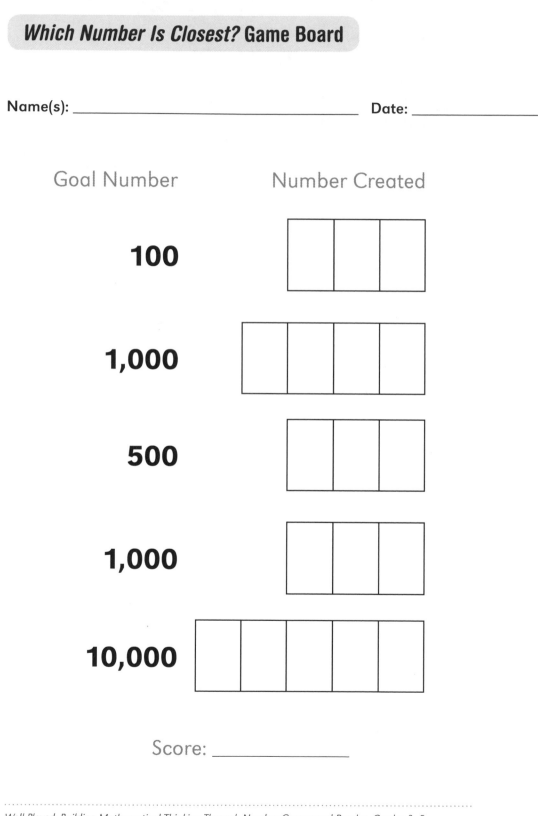

Goal Number   Number Created

100

1,000

500

1,000

10,000

Score: _____

Which Number Is Closest? Cards

> Make two copies of these cards to form one deck.

0	1	2	3
4	5	6	7
8	9		

Which Number Is Closest? Directions

Materials Needed

> 1 *Which Number Is Closest?* Game Board per team (page A-4)
> 1 deck of *Which Number Is Closest?* Cards (made from *two* copies of page A-5) per group of players
> Optional: 1 *Which Number Is Closest?* Directions per group

Directions

Goal: Place digits in the spaces to form numbers as close in value as possible to the goal numbers.

> Shuffle the cards and place them facedown. Choose a player to be the game leader.
> The game leader turns over one card and announces the number. Each team writes the digit in one of the spaces (boxes) in the "Number Created" column of the game board.
> All teams must record the digit before the next number is announced, and once written, its placement may not be changed.
> The leader continues turning over cards until eighteen digits have been placed. (Note that the last two cards will not be used.)
> Compare how close each of the teams' numbers is to each goal number. The team with the closest number wins a point. Each team adds its points to find its score. The team with the most points wins the game.

The Number Is/What Number Is? Cards

The number is 236,427. *What number is* 250 tens and 3 ones?	The number is 2,503. *What number is* 50,000 + 700 + 3?	The number is 50,703. *What number is* rounded to 2,500 when rounded to the nearest hundred?	The number is 2,489. *What number is* greater than 350 thousands?
The number is 405,786. *What number is* 2,000 more than 10,000?	The number is 12,000. *What number is* 17 hundreds and 15 tens?	The number is 1,715. *What number is* less than 2,000?	The number is 1,850. *What number is* one more than 15,699?
The number is fifteen thousand seven hundred. *What number is* between 10,000 and 14,000?	The number is 13,700. *What number is* rounded to 25,000 when rounded to the nearest thousand?	The number is 25,499. *What number is* 200,000 + 40,000 + 7?	The number is two hundred forty thousand seven. *What number is* 10,000 + 400 + 30 + 6?
The number is ten thousand four hundred thirty-six. *What number is* 72 hundreds?	The number is 7,200. *What number is* 2,000 + 500 + 60 + 3?	The number is 2,563. *What number is* between 70 tens and 80 tens?	The number is 742. *What number is* less than 800?
The number is 450. *What number is* 63 thousands, 25 hundreds, 18 ones?	The number is 65,518. *What number is* greater than half a million?	The number is 827,345. *What number* rounds to 20,000 when rounded to the nearest ten thousand?	The number is 18,239. *What number is* rounded to 200,000 when rounded to the nearest hundred thousand?

The Number Is/What Number Is?
Cards to Make Your Own Puzzle

The number is What number is	The number is What number is	The number is What number is	The number is What number is
The number is What number is	The number is What number is	The number is What number is	The number is What number is
The number is What number is	The number is What number is	The number is What number is	The number is What number is
The number is What number is	The number is What number is	The number is What number is	The number is What number is
The number is What number is	The number is What number is	The number is What number	The number is What number is

The Number Is/What Number Is? Directions

Materials Needed

> 1 deck of *The Number Is/What Number Is?* Cards per group of two to four students (page A-7)
> Optional: 1 set of *The Number Is/What Number Is?* Cards to Make Your Own Puzzle per pair of students (page A-8)
> Optional: 1 *The Number Is/What Number Is?* Directions per group

Directions

Goal: Place cards so that the number identified on each card answers the question on the card before it.

> Spread out the cards faceup on a table or the floor.
> Choose a card and read its question.
> Find a card with a matching answer, place this card next to the first card, and read the question on this second card.
> Continue to read questions and find answers. Organize the cards in a circle so that each question is followed with a correct answer.
> Each card must be included in the circle.

Mystery Number Recording Sheet

Name(s): _____ Date: _____

The range for this game is _____ to _____.

Questions Asked	What We Know Now

Mystery Number Directions

Materials Needed

› 1 *Mystery Number* Recording Sheet per team (page A-10)
› Optional: 1 *Mystery Number* Directions per group of four students

Directions

Goal: Ask questions that can be answered with *yes* or *no* to identify the mystery number.

› Decide which team will choose the mystery number and which team will try to guess it. The team choosing the mystery number also identifies a range of numbers it is between, for example, between 500 and 800 or between 0.46 and 0.875. A player on this team privately writes down the number and range and begins the game by saying, "The mystery number is between …," and naming the range of numbers.

› Players on the other team ask questions that can be answered only with *yes* or *no*, such as *Is the number even?* These players record questions and conclusions on the team's recording sheet.

› Questions are asked until a player identifies the answer by posing a question such as *Is the number 4.7?* and having the other team respond *yes* and share what was recorded at the beginning of the game.

Get to One Hundredths Game Board

0.01	0.02	0.03	0.04	0.05	0.06	0.07	0.08	0.09	0.10
0.11	0.12	0.13	0.14	0.15	0.16	0.17	0.18	0.19	0.20
0.21	0.22	0.23	0.24	0.25	0.26	0.27	0.28	0.29	0.30
0.31	0.32	0.33	0.34	0.35	0.36	0.37	0.38	0.39	0.40
0.41	0.42	0.43	0.44	0.45	0.46	0.47	0.48	0.49	0.50
0.51	0.52	0.53	0.54	0.55	0.56	0.57	0.58	0.59	0.60
0.61	0.62	0.63	0.64	0.65	0.66	0.67	0.68	0.69	0.70
0.71	0.72	0.73	0.74	0.75	0.76	0.77	0.78	0.79	0.80
0.81	0.82	0.83	0.84	0.85	0.86	0.87	0.88	0.89	0.90
0.91	0.92	0.93	0.94	0.95	0.96	0.97	0.98	0.99	1.00

Get to One-Tenth Thousandths Game Board

0.001	0.002	0.003	0.004	0.005	0.006	0.007	0.008	0.009	0.010
0.011	0.012	0.013	0.014	0.015	0.016	0.017	0.018	0.019	0.020
0.021	0.022	0.023	0.024	0.025	0.026	0.027	0.028	0.029	0.030
0.031	0.032	0.033	0.034	0.035	0.036	0.037	0.038	0.039	0.040
0.041	0.042	0.043	0.044	0.045	0.046	0.047	0.048	0.049	0.050
0.051	0.052	0.053	0.054	0.055	0.056	0.057	0.058	0.059	0.060
0.061	0.062	0.063	0.064	0.065	0.066	0.067	0.068	0.069	0.070
0.071	0.072	0.073	0.074	0.075	0.076	0.077	0.078	0.079	0.080
0.081	0.082	0.083	0.084	0.085	0.086	0.087	0.088	0.089	0.090
0.091	0.092	0.093	0.094	0.095	0.096	0.097	0.098	0.099	0.100

Get to One or One-Tenth Recording Sheet

Name(s): _____   Date: _____

I am playing Get to _____ .

We rolled _____. We give it the value of _____. Now we are at _____.

We rolled _____. We give it the value of _____. Now we are at _____.

We rolled _____. We give it the value of _____. Now we are at _____.

We rolled _____. We give it the value of _____. Now we are at _____.

We rolled _____. We give it the value of _____. Now we are at _____.

We rolled _____. We give it the value of _____. Now we are at _____.

We rolled _____. We give it the value of _____. Now we are at _____.

We rolled _____. We give it the value of _____. Now we are at _____.

We rolled _____. We give it the value of _____. Now we are at _____.

We rolled _____. We give it the value of _____. Now we are at _____.

We rolled _____. We give it the value of _____. Now we are at _____.

We rolled _____. We give it the value of _____. Now we are at _____.

We rolled _____. We give it the value of _____. Now we are at _____.

We rolled _____. We give it the value of _____. Now we are at _____.

We rolled _____. We give it the value of _____. Now we are at _____.

We rolled _____. We give it the value of _____. Now we are at _____.

Get to One or One-Tenth Directions

Materials Needed
› 1 die per team
› 1 chip per team
› 1 *Get to One* Hundredths Game Board (page A-12) or *Get to One-Tenth* Thousandths Game Board (page A-13) per team
› 1 *Get to One or One-Tenth* Recording Sheet per team (page A-14)
› Optional: 1 *Get to One or One-Tenth* Directions per group

Directions
Goal: Move forward on the game board by tenths or hundredths (or thousandths) to reach 1.00 (or 0.1).

› Decide which team goes first.
› On each turn, a team's representative rolls the die and talks with the team about whether to have the number represent tenths or hundredths (or hundredths or thousandths). That number is then counted on the hundredths (or thousandths) board, starting at 0. Players can indicate their position by counting and placing a chip on the final number.
› Alternate turns, with each team counting on from its last number.
› If a team cannot fully complete a count, for example, the team is on 0.97 and rolls a 4, the turn is lost.
› The first team to reach 1.00 (or 0.1) wins the game.

Well Played: Building Mathematical Thinking Through Number Games and Puzzles, Grades 3–5
by Linda Dacey, Karen Gartland, and Jayne Bamford Lynch. Copyright © 2015. Stenhouse Publishers.

Can You Make This Number? Game Board

Name(s): _____   Date: _____

Game A

Descriptions	Roll	Number
a. Greater than 32 thousands	_____	____ ____ , ____ ____ ____
b. 2 in the hundreds place	_____	____ ____ , ____ ____ ____
c. Rounds to 31,000 when rounded to the nearest thousand	_____	____ ____ , ____ ____ ____
d. Less than 20,000 + 400 + 3	_____	____ ____ , ____ ____ ____
e. 1 in the hundreds place and 4 in the thousands place	_____	____ ____ , ____ ____ ____
f. Between 43 thousands and 51 thousands	_____	____ ____ , ____ ____ ____

Game B

Descriptions	Roll	Number
a. Less than 24	_____	____ ____ , ____ ____ ____
b. 3 in the hundredths place and 6 in the thousandths place	_____	____ ____ , ____ ____ ____
c. Greater than 45.214	_____	____ ____ , ____ ____ ____
d. Less than 25 + 0.3 + 0.56	_____	____ ____ , ____ ____ ____
e. 1 in the thousandths place and 3 in the tenths place	_____	____ ____ , ____ ____ ____
f. Rounds to 52.4 when rounded to the nearest tenth	_____	____ ____ , ____ ____ ____

Can You Make This Number? Directions

Materials Needed

› 5 dice per group of four students
› 1 *Can You Make This Number?* Game Board A or B per team (page A-16, top or bottom half)
› Optional: 1 *Can You Make This Number?* Directions per group

Directions

Goal: Roll dice and use the numbers rolled as digits to try to form numbers to meet the given descriptions.

› One pair of students alternates turns with another pair of students.
› On its first turn, Team 1 rolls five dice and talks about how to use each of the numbers rolled as digits to form a number that can fit the first description on the game board.
› If the team can make a number to fit the description, it records the number and gives the dice to Team 2. On its next turn, Team 1 will try to make a number to fit the next description.
› If the team cannot make a number to fit the description, its turn ends and the team gives the dice to Team 2. Team 1 must roll and try again to meet the first description on its next turn.
› The teams continue to alternate turns, trying to make the numbers described in the order they appear on the game board.
› The first team to make all six numbers wins the game.

What's Your Problem? Game Board

Name(s): _____ Date: _____

The Knower Board

Line 1   _____ _____ _____

Line 2   +   _____ _____ _____
_____
Line 3   _____ _____ _____ _____

Name(s): _____ Date: _____

The Guesser Board

Line 1   _____ _____ _____

Line 2   +   _____ _____ _____
_____
Line 3   _____ _____ _____ _____

What's Your Problem? Directions

Materials Needed

› 1 *What's Your Problem?* Game Board per team (page A-18)
› Optional: 1 *What's Your Problem?* Directions per group

Directions

Goal: Identify all the digits in a mystery problem within fifteen guesses.

› Take turns being the "knower" and the "guesser" teams. Use different parts of your game board as you do so.

› The knower team creates and solves an addition problem involving two three-digit numbers on the knower part of the board, taking care to compute accurately.

› The guesser team asks questions in the following format: *Are there any _____s in the _____ column?* For example, the guesser might ask, "Are there any 3s in the ones column?"

› If the guesser team is correct about the number *and* the column, the knower team answers by telling which line in that column the number is on. If there is more than one such number in the column, the knower team identifies all of them. The guesser team records this information on its game board.

› If the guesser team is incorrect about *either* the number or the column, the knower team says, "No, there is no 3 in the ones column." To keep track of the number of guesses used, a guesser team player marks an *x* on one of the fifteen lines below the computation example for each question his or her team asks.

› A guesser player may ask, "Is there a 4 in the ones column and a 2 in the tens column?" If both parts of the guess are not correct, the answer will be "No."

› If the guesser team does not figure out the computation problem within fifteen questions, the knower team reveals the answer and the teams exchange roles.

Well Played: Building Mathematical Thinking Through Number Games and Puzzles, Grades 3–5
by Linda Dacey, Karen Gartland, and Jayne Bamford Lynch. Copyright © 2015. Stenhouse Publishers.

Tic-Tic-Tac-Toe Game 1 Game Board

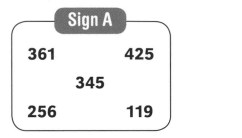

Sign A

361		425
	345	
256		119

Sign B

47		175
	516	
269		56

408	294	941	525	401
520	694	312	877	303
772	175	536	392	388
417	472	614	431	635
630	861	166	481	600

Tic-Tic-Tac-Toe Game 2 Game Board

Sign A		
1,854		4,941
	5,145	
6,372		2,632

Sign B		
10,346		9,641
	11,887	
12,440		8,789

12,200	13,741	10,643	11,495	14,294
16,828	12,273	15,287	17,381	13,730
13,934	15,491	17,585	14,519	14,786
16,013	18,812	18,259	15,161	16,718
15,072	11,421	14,582	12,978	17,032

Tic-Tic-Tac-Toe Directions

Materials Needed

› 1 *Tic-Tic-Tac-Toe* Game 1 or Game 2 Game Board per group of players (page A-20 or A-21)
› Optional: 1 *Tic-Tic-Tac-Toe* Directions per group

Directions

Goal: Choose addends in order to mark off four sums in a row, column, or diagonal on the game board.

› Decide which team will be X and which will be O. The first team picks a number from Sign A and one from Sign B. Both teams compute the sum. (Teams get to pick only once, even if they discover that they don't get a sum they want.)
› Once both teams have confirmed the sum, the first team finds it on the game board and writes the team's mark (*X* or *O*) in that space.
› If the team gets a sum that is already marked with an *X* or an *O*, it loses its turn.
› Teams alternate turns.
› The first team to write its mark in four touching sums in a row, column, or diagonal is the winner. These *X*'s are in the same row and touch:

These *X*'s are in the same row but do not all touch:

Logical Numbers Puzzle A

Name(s): _____ Date: _____

Five friends are running in a race to raise money to build a new playground.
Their race bib numbers are 337, 135, 142, 632, and 545.
Use the clues to find the number each racer is wearing.

1. The sum of Mica's and Cooper's race numbers is an even number.
2. If you add Isabella's race number to itself, the sum is 674.
3. If you subtract Jordana's race number from Mica's race number, the difference is greater than 200.
4. The difference between Jordana's race number and Isabella's race number is less than 200.
5. Riley's race number is equal to $906 - 342 + 68$.

Names					

Race Numbers

The race number for Mica is _____.

The race number Cooper for is _____.

The race number for Isabella is _____.

The race number for Riley is _____.

The race number for Jordana is _____.

Well Played: Building Mathematical Thinking Through Number Games and Puzzles, Grades 3–5
by Linda Dacey, Karen Gartland, and Jayne Bamford Lynch. Copyright © 2015. Stenhouse Publishers.

Logical Numbers Puzzle B

Name(s): _____   Date: _____

Ms. Miller has six codes she has to remember.
The code numbers are 2902; 7987; 4269; 11440; 4149; and 15302.
Use the clues to find what each code opens.

1. The code number for the front door subtracted from the code number for the computer is equal to the code number for the safe added to the code number for the front door.
2. If you wrote the code number for the car three times and found the sum of these numbers, it would be 12,447.
3. The code number for the computer is not equal to 11,070 – 8,295 + 127.
4. The code number for the computer minus the code number for the back door is 3,453.
5. The code for the combination lock is equal to 11,569 + 5,742 – 2,009.

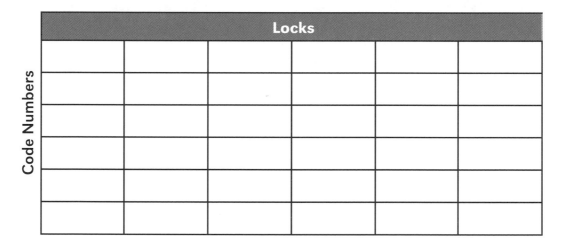

The code number for the computer is _____.

The code number for the front door is _____.

The code number for the back door is _____.

The code number for the safe is _____.

The code number for the car is _____.

The code number for the combination lock is _____.

Logical Numbers Directions

Materials Needed

› 1 *Logical Numbers* Puzzle A or B per student or pair (page A-23 or A-24)
› Optional: 1 *Logical Numbers* Directions per student or pair
› Optional: 1 calculator per student

Directions

Goal: Use the clues to match the right pieces of information with each other (for example, race bib numbers with racers and codes with types of locks).

› Work alone or with a partner.
› Read the clues.
› Use the table to organize what you know from each clue.
› Make notes so that you can recall your thinking. Include computation and clue numbers in your notes.
› You do not need to use the clues in order.
› Check your solution with each clue.

Subtracto Draw Game Board

Name(s): _____   Date: _____

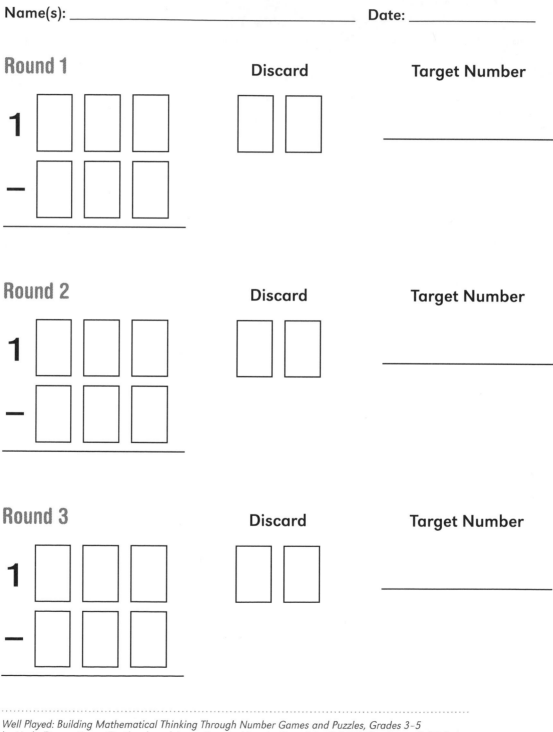

Round 1

Discard

Target Number
_____

Round 2

Discard

Target Number
_____

Round 3

Discard

Target Number
_____

Subtracto Draw Cards

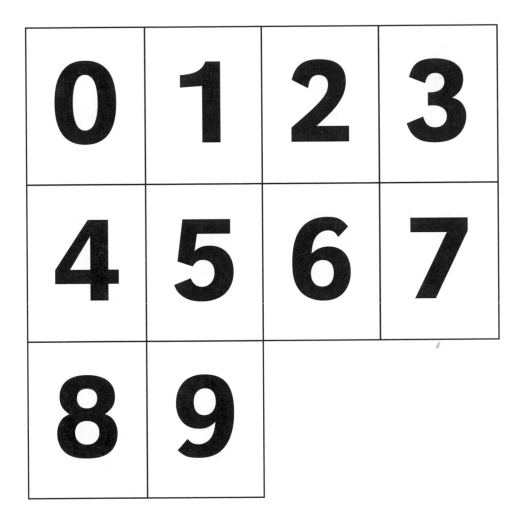

Subtracto Draw Directions

Materials Needed

> 1 *Subtracto Draw* Game Board per team (page A-26)
> 1 deck of *Subtracto Draw* Cards per group of players (page A-27)
> Optional: 1 *Subtracto Draw* Directions per group

Directions

Goal: Place digits to create a subtraction example with a difference closest to the target number.

> Shuffle the cards and place them facedown. Choose one student to be the card turner. That student turns over the top three cards to form a three-digit number. Each team writes this number on its recording sheet as the target number for the round.
> Place those three cards back in the deck and shuffle the cards again.
> The card turner turns over the top card of the deck, and each team decides privately where to write the number in the subtraction example for round 1 or to write it in the discard area. Once the team has written a number, it can't move the number to another space.
> Turn over the next card and decide where to place that digit.
> After eight cards have been turned over and recorded, teams subtract to find their differences.
> Teams exchange papers to check each other's subtraction.
> Teams then return papers and determine together which team found a difference closest to the target number. That team gets a point for that round.
> After three rounds, the team with more points wins.

Double Decimal Dilemma Recording Sheet

Name(s): _____   Date: _____

	Points for Round	Total Points
Round 1		
Round 2		
Round 3		
Round 4		
Round 5		
Round 6		
Round 7		
Round 8		

Double Decimal Dilemma Directions

Materials Needed

› 2 dice per group of players
› 1 calculator per group
› 1 *Double Decimal Dilemma* Recording Sheet per team (page A-29)
› Optional: 1 *Double Decimal Dilemma* Directions per group

Directions

Goal: Roll dice and use mental computation to reach a total score of 15 (or more).

› You will be rolling dice and finding the sum of the numbers you roll. The numbers on the dice represent tenths. For example, if you roll a 1, that represents 0.1.

› Take turns. On each turn you should roll the two dice and find their sum. Continue rolling and adding each new sum, using mental arithmetic, to your previous total.

› End your turn by handing the dice to your opponent when
  › you decide it's best to end your turn to secure your score;
  › your opponent correctly challenges your mental arithmetic, which requires you to end your turn and go back to the mental sum you acquired before your error (challenges can be checked with calculators); or
  › you roll doubles, which means you lose your turn and your score for this round returns to 0.

› After each turn, record the total for this round, which remains part of your total score no matter what happens on your future turns, and find and record your running total.

› The game ends when one team reaches a score of 15 or more.

Well Played: Building Mathematical Thinking Through Number Games and Puzzles, Grades 3–5
by Linda Dacey, Karen Gartland, and Jayne Bamford Lynch. Copyright © 2015. Stenhouse Publishers.

Table Topper Game Board

1	2	3	4	5	6	7	8	9
2	4	6	8	10	12	14	16	18
3	6	9	12	15	18	21	24	27
4	8	12	16	20	24	28	32	36
5	10	15	20	25	30	35	40	45
6	12	18	24	30	36	42	48	54
7	14	21	28	35	42	49	56	63
8	16	24	32	40	48	56	64	72
9	18	27	36	45	54	63	72	81

Factors

1	2	3	4	5	6	7	8	9

Table Topper Directions

Materials Needed

› 1 die per group of players
› 2 large paper clips per group
› 1 *Table Topper* Game Board per group (page A-31)
› Optional: 1 *Table Topper* Directions per group

Directions

Goal: Multiply factors to get four products in a row, column, or diagonal on the game board.

› Choose which team will use *X*'s and which will use *O*'s.
› For the first round of play, the opposing team puts a paper clip on one of the factors 1–9, shown at the bottom of the game board. Then the team that is playing first also places its clip on one of the factors. (It may be the same number chosen by the other team or a different number.) The playing team multiplies these two numbers, finds their product in the multiplication table, and "tops" it by writing its symbol, *X* or *O*, on it.
› After this first round, teams alternate turns. On each turn, the playing team moves *either one* of the paper clips to a new factor, multiplies these factors, and writes *X* or *O* on top of the product.
› The first team to have four *X*'s or *O*'s beside each other in a row, column, or diagonal wins.

Five of a Kind Factor Cards

8 × ___ = 48	3 × ___ = 18
9 × ___ = 54	4 × ___ = 24
3 × ___ = 21	5 × ___ = 30
4 × ___ = 28	6 × ___ = 36
5 × ___ = 35	7 × ___ = 42

Five of a Kind Factor Cards (continued)

$6 \times \underline{} = 42$	$4 \times \underline{} = 32$
$7 \times \underline{} = 49$	$5 \times \underline{} = 40$
$8 \times \underline{} = 56$	$6 \times \underline{} = 48$
$9 \times \underline{} = 63$	$7 \times \underline{} = 56$
$3 \times \underline{} = 24$	$8 \times \underline{} = 64$

Five of a Kind Factor Cards (continued)

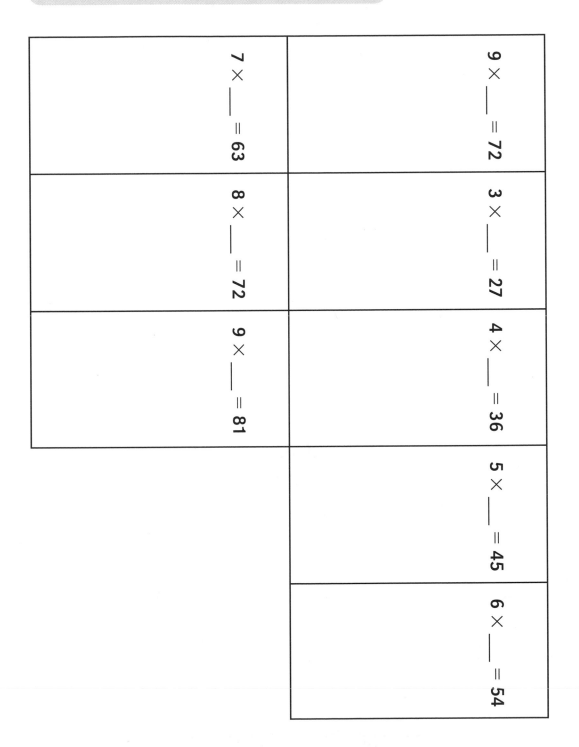

9 × ___ = 72	7 × ___ = 63
3 × ___ = 27	8 × ___ = 72
4 × ___ = 36	9 × ___ = 81
5 × ___ = 45	
6 × ___ = 54	

Five of a Kind Quotient Cards

$18 \div 3 =$ ___	$48 \div 8 =$ ___
$24 \div 4 =$ ___	$54 \div 9 =$ ___
$30 \div 5 =$ ___	$21 \div 3 =$ ___
$36 \div 6 =$ ___	$28 \div 4 =$ ___
$42 \div 7 =$ ___	$35 \div 5 =$ ___

Five of a Kind Quotient Cards (continued)

42 ÷ 6 = __	32 ÷ 4 = __
49 ÷ 7 = __	40 ÷ 5 = __
56 ÷ 8 = __	48 ÷ 6 = __
63 ÷ 9 = __	56 ÷ 7 = __
24 ÷ 3 = __	64 ÷ 8 = __

Five of a Kind Quotient Cards (continued)

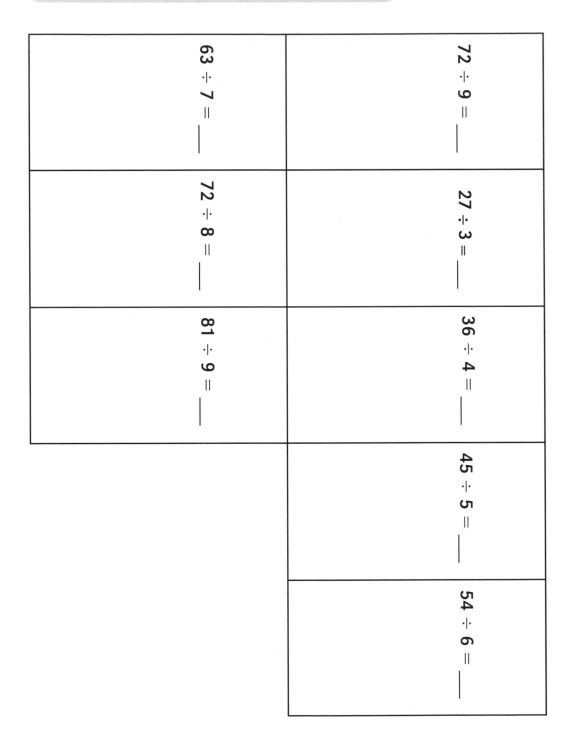

$72 \div 9 =$ _____

$63 \div 7 =$ _____

$27 \div 3 =$ _____

$72 \div 8 =$ _____

$36 \div 4 =$ _____

$81 \div 9 =$ _____

$45 \div 5 =$ _____

$54 \div 6 =$ _____

Five of a Kind Directions

Materials Needed

› 1 deck of *Five of a Kind* Factor or Quotient Cards A or B, made from five cards with the same missing factor per group of four players (pages A-33–A-35 or pages A-36–A-38)
› Optional: 1 *Five of a Kind* Directions per group

Directions

Goal: Collect five playing cards with equations that have the same missing factor.

› Four players sit in a circle.
› Sort the cards by putting cards with the same missing factor (or quotient) in the same pile. Choose five cards from each pile to use in the game. Put the other cards aside.
› Shuffle the cards.
› Deal five cards to each player.
› At the same time, each player looks at his or her own cards and decides on one card the player does not want. The player places that card facedown in front of the player to the right. All the players pick up their new cards so that each person once again has five cards in his or her hand.
› Players continue to pass and pick up cards, waiting for all players to pick up before the next pass begins.
› The first player to get five cards with equations that have the same missing factor says, "Five of a kind!" and wins.

Equal Values Cards

=	=
3×8	8×3
8×7	$5 \times 7 + 3 \times 7$
$6 \times 2 \times 5$	6×10
$4 \times 3 + 4 \times 3$	8×3
9×6	$10 \times 6 - 6$
9×8	8×9
$2 \times 7 + 3 \times 7$	5×7

Equal Values Cards (continued)

34×6	6×34
23×4	$20 \times 4 + 3 \times 4$
$20 \times 7 \times 5$	7×100
$50 \times 18 \times 2$	100×18
578×5	5×578
$40 \times 9 \times 5$	200×9
395×5	$400 \times 5 - 5 \times 5$
$2 \times 250 \times 5$	250×10

Equal Values Cards (continued)

540×6	$500 \times 6 + 40 \times 6$
699×4	$700 \times 4 - 4$
$17 \times 5 \times 2$	17×10
$2 \times 18 + 2 \times 18$	18×4
98×5	$100 \times 5 - 2 \times 5$
$20 \times 6 \times 5$	6×100
23×4	$20 \times 4 + 3 \times 4$
$17 \times 5 \times 2$	17×10

Equal Values Recording Sheet

Name(s): _____ Date: _____

Card #1	Card #2	How do you know the cards make a pack?

Equal Values Directions

Materials Needed

> 1 deck of *Equal Values* Cards per group of four students (pages A-40–A-42)
> 1 *Equal Values* Recording Sheet per group (page A-43)
> Optional: 1 *Equal Values* Directions per group
> Optional: 1 calculator

Directions

Goal: Get more pairs of cards that have equal values.

> Give each team a card with the equal sign.
> Shuffle the cards. Deal each team four cards faceup for all to see. Put the other cards facedown in a pile.
> On each turn you can do one of three things:
>   1. Find two of your cards that have an equal value. Set this pack beside you. Replace them with two cards from the top of the pile.
>   2. Trade one of your cards with one of the other team's cards when you are able to make a pack. Set this pack beside you. Replace your card with a card from the top of the pile.
>   3. Draw a card from the top of the pile and add it to your cards.
> When a pack is made, both teams must agree on the product and then one player records their thinking.
> If no cards are left in the deck, you can still have a turn, but you don't take a card.
> The game ends when no team can make another pack.
> The team with more packs wins.

Think Remainder Game Board

11	12	13	15
17	18	19	20
21	23	24	27
29	31	32	35
42	44	47	49

Think Remainder Recording Sheet

Name(s): _____ Date: _____

I/We Rolled	Number Crossed Out	Related Fact	Remainder
Total score:			

Think Remainder Directions

Materials Needed

› 1 die per group of players
› 1 *Think Remainder* Game Board per group (page A-45)
› 1 *Think Remainder* Recording Sheet per team (page A-46)
› Optional: 1 *Think Remainder* Directions per group

Directions

Goal: Have the greater sum when adding the remainders of ten division examples.

› Take turns. When it's your team's turn, your team is known as the "rolling team."
› A member of the rolling team rolls the die.
› A member of the opposing team crosses out a number on the game board.
› Players on the rolling team divide the number crossed out by the number rolled. The remainder is the rolling team's score for this turn. A member of the team records the numbers for this turn on the team's recording sheet.
› Teams take turns rolling, crossing out numbers, dividing, and recording the work for this turn. (Crossed-out numbers cannot be used again.)
› When every number on the board has been crossed out, teams compare their total scores by adding all the remainders from their turns.
› The team with the greater score wins.

Matchups Puzzle A

Name(s): _____ Date: _____

Write each factor below one of its multiples. The factor cannot be the same number as the multiple you choose. You must write each factor exactly once and write a number on each line.

Factor List

1	2	3	5	7
8	9	10	25	

Multiple Board

11	80	45
_____	_____	_____
32	15	21
_____	_____	_____
50	4	10
_____	_____	_____

Matchups Puzzle B

Name(s): _____ Date: _____

Write each factor below one of its multiples. The factor cannot be the same number as the multiple you choose. You must write each factor exactly once and write a number on each line.

Factor List

1	2	3	4	5	6	7	8
10	11	12	15	17	31	48	70

Multiple Board

21	310	144	6
___	___	___	___
100	13	25	700
___	___	___	___
54	49	150	72
___	___	___	___
70	33	34	64
___	___	___	___

Well Played: Building Mathematical Thinking Through Number Games and Puzzles, Grades 3–5
by Linda Dacey, Karen Gartland, and Jayne Bamford Lynch. Copyright © 2015. Stenhouse Publishers.

Matchups Directions

Materials Needed

› 1 *Matchups* Puzzle A or B per pair of students (page A-48 or A-49)
› Optional: 1 *Matchups* Directions per pair

Directions

Goal: Using each factor only once, match each given factor with exactly one given multiple.

› Each number in the factor list is a factor of one or more of the numbers on the multiple board.
› Write each factor on a blank beneath one of its multiples on the board. The factor cannot be the same number as the multiple you choose. Each factor must be written exactly once.
› Write the factors so that each multiple gets a match.

Roll Six Recording Sheet

Name(s): _____   Date: _____

	Rolled	Product
1		
2		
3		
4		
5		
6		

Use the products to complete the equations. A product may be used only once in a particular equation. Not all of the products must be included in each equation.

_____ = 1

_____ = 2

_____ = 3

_____ = 4

_____ = 5

_____ = 6

You score 1 point for each equation that is recorded accurately.

Score: _____

Roll Six Directions

Materials Needed

> 1 die per group of players
> 1 three-minute timer per group
> 1 *Roll Six* Recording Sheet per team (page A-51)
> Optional: 1 *Roll Six* Directions per group

Directions

Goal: Roll numbers on a die, use them in a table to find products, and then use the products to write expressions equal to each of the numbers one through six.

> For the first part of the game, opponents work together to complete the table at the top of their recording sheets. To begin, a player on one team rolls the die and that team decides where, in the second column of the table, the number will be recorded. Both teams then record the number and the product of the two numbers in that row. For example, if the team rolls a 6 and places it in the column beside the 2, it records 12 in the third column.

> Teams take turns rolling and deciding where the number will be recorded until the table is completed.

> Next, a player starts the timer and teams have three minutes to use these products to privately create equations with the values 1 through 6. So if the players have the products 3, 8, 18, 20, 5, and 36, then each team uses these numbers to complete equations with values of 1, 2, 3, 4, 5, and 6. A product may not be used more than once in a single equation. Not all of the products have to be included in each equation.

> When the time is up, teams share their equations and check each other's work for accuracy. Teams get a point for each of the numbers one through six for which they could write an accurate equation. The team with the greater number of points wins. (If each team gets the same number of points, it is a tie.)

Write It Right Puzzle A

Name(s): _____ Date: _____

Use each of the digits 0, 1, 2, 3, 4, 5, 6, 7, 8, and 9 exactly once in the set of equations. The math must make sense.

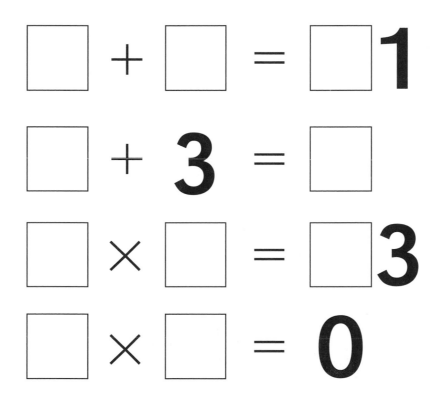

Ideas that helped eliminate some of the choices:

Write It Right Puzzle B

Name(s): _____ Date: _____

Use each of the digits 0, 1, 2, 3, 4, 5, 6, 7, 8, and 9 exactly once in each puzzle. The math must make sense.

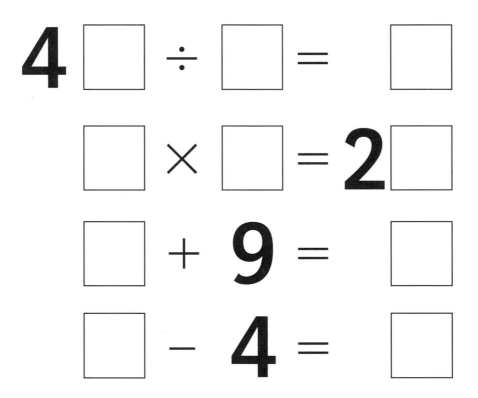

Ideas that helped eliminate some of the choices:

Write It Right Puzzle C

Name(s): _____ Date: _____

Place each number in one box below so that the puzzle makes sense.

0.1   0.2   0.3   0.4   0.5   0.6   4   6   10   100

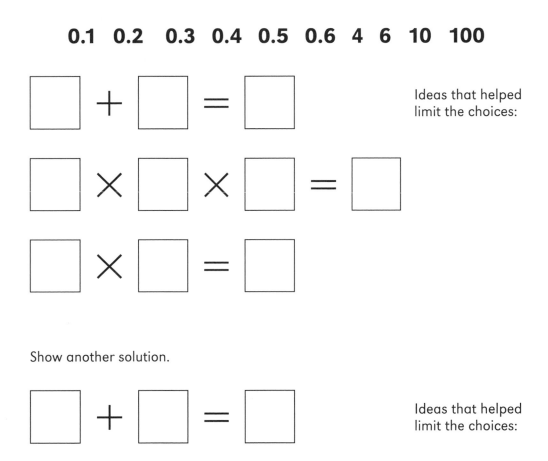

Ideas that helped
limit the choices:

Show another solution.

Ideas that helped
limit the choices:

Write It Right Directions

Materials Needed

> 1 *Write It Right* Puzzle A, B, or C per pair of students (page A-53, A-54, or A-55)
> Optional: 1 *Write It Right* Directions per pair

Directions

Goal: Write the given numbers in the puzzle so that all the equations are true.

> Use each of the given numbers exactly once in the puzzle.
> The equations must be true.
> Check to make sure each equation is correct.
> Identify ideas that helped you decide where to write the numbers.

Decade Roll Recording Sheet

Name(s): _____ Date: _____

Numbers rolled: _____, _____, _____, _____

Equations created:

0–9: _____

10–19: _____

20–29: _____

30–39: _____

40–49: _____

50–59: _____

60–69: _____

70–79: _____

80–89: _____

90–99: _____

Decade Roll Directions

Materials Needed

› 4 dice per group of players
› 1 two-minute timer per group
› 1 *Decade Roll* Recording Sheet per team (page A-57)
› Optional: 1 *Decade Roll* Directions per group
› Optional: 1 calculator per group

Directions

Goal: Roll dice and use each of the numbers shown to write expressions equal to a number in each of the decades ones through nineties.

› Choose one student to roll four dice.
› Each team has two minutes to privately use the numbers rolled to make expressions that equal numbers in each decade from the ones to the nineties. Each expression must use each of the numbers rolled exactly once. The numbers can be used as single digits or be combined to form two- or three-digit numbers.
› You may use any of the four operations in the equations. More than one operation may be used. So if you rolled dice showing the numbers 4, 5, 1, and 6 and wanted to write an equation for a number in the teens, possibilities would include $4 + 5 + 1 + 6 = 16$; $61 - 45 = 16$; $4 \times 5 - 1 - 6 = 13$; and $5 + 1 \times 6 + 4 = 15$.
› Write the equations on the *Decade Roll* Recording Sheet. Be sure to include parentheses if needed.
› When the time is finished, trade papers, and check each other's equations. The winner is the team with the greater number of correct equations.

Calculator Target Cards

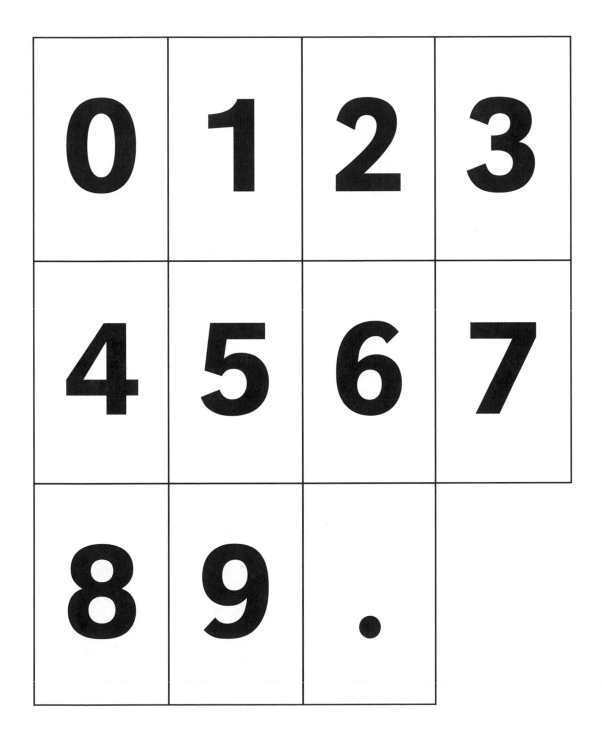

Calculator Target Recording Sheet

Name(s): _____ Date: _____

Round 1

Target Number: _____

_____ ▢ _____ = _____   Points _____

Round 2

Target Number: _____

_____ ▢ _____ = _____   Points _____

Round 3

Target Number: _____

_____ ▢ _____ = _____   Points _____

Round 4

Target number: _____

_____ ▢ _____ = _____   Points _____

Round 5

Target number: _____

_____ ▢ _____ = _____   Points _____

Total points: _____

Calculator Target Directions

Materials Needed

› 1 calculator per team
› 1 deck of *Calculator Target* Cards per group (decimal point card is optional) (page A-59)
› 1 *Calculator Target* Recording Sheet per team (page A-60)
› 1 *Calculator Target* Directions per group

Directions

Goal: Complete expressions to meet or get close to the target numbers.

› Shuffle the deck of *Calculator Target* cards and place them facedown.
› Team 1 turns over the top three cards of the deck and uses the numbers to form a three-digit number. This number is the target number for round 1, and both teams should write it on their recording sheets.
› Teams exchange recording sheets, and opposing teams record an operation sign in the square for round 1 and a number that is less than the target number in the blank immediately to the right of that sign.
› Teams return recording sheets, and without using paper and pencil or a calculator, each team quickly writes a number in the blank to the left of the operational sign.
› Teams then use their calculators to complete the equations.
› Each team determines its points for this round by finding the difference between its answer and the target number, subtracting from the greater number. Each team records its points for this round.
› Reshuffle the cards. Team 2 turns three cards over and forms the target number for round 2, and teams once again exchange recording sheets.
› Teams continue to alternate forming the three-digit numbers for five rounds. Then teams find their total points. The team with the fewer number of points wins.

Contig Game Board

1	2	3	4	5	6	7	8
9	10	11	12	13	14	15	16
17	18	19	20	21	22	23	24
25	26	27	28	29	30	31	32
33	34	35	36	37	38	39	40
41	42	44	45	48	50	54	55
60	64	66	72	75	80	90	96
100	108	120	125	144	150	180	216

Contig Recording Sheet

Name(s): _____ Date: _____

Round 1: We rolled _____, _____, _____

Our equation: _____ Points _____

Points received on our opponent's turn Points _____

Round 2: We rolled _____, _____, _____

Our equation: _____ Points _____

Points received on our opponent's turn Points _____

Round 3: We rolled _____, _____, _____

Our equation: _____ Points _____

Points received on our opponent's turn Points _____

Round 4:

We rolled _____, _____, _____

Our equation: _____ Points _____

Points received on our opponent's turn Points _____

Round 5:

We rolled _____, _____, _____

Our equation: _____ Points _____

Points received on our opponent's turn Points _____

Round 6: We rolled _____, _____, _____

Our equation: _____ Points _____

Points received on our opponent's turn Points _____

Total score: _____

Contig Directions

Materials Needed
› 3 dice per group of players
› 1 *Contig* Game Board per group (page A-62)
› 1 *Contig* Recording Sheet per team (page A-63)
› Optional: 1 *Contig* Directions per group

Directions
Goal: Use numbers rolled on three dice to write expressions equal to numbers on the game board, getting points for those numbers and any numbers they touch.

› Each team selects a player to roll a die. The team with the lesser number plays first.
› Take turns.
› On each turn you roll three dice and use each of the numbers exactly once, along with any of the four operations, to write an expression. You can use more than one operation or use the same operation twice.
› Simplify your expression and confirm the accuracy with your opponent.
› Look for the answer on the *Contig* Game Board and if it is not already marked, mark it with an *X*. This number may not be marked again. Write your equation on the *Contig* Recording Sheet.
› You get 1 point for creating an expression equal to an unmarked number on the board and 1 point for each other *marked* number next to it (in a row, column, or diagonal).
› If the opposing team can create an expression with the same numbers that's worth more points, it gets the additional points. If you can't find a solution on your turn, and the other team can, that team gets all those points. In either case, the opposing team's number is not marked.
› So in the mini-board shown below, if you could mark 29, you would receive 2 points: 1 point for 29 and 1 for 21, as it touches 29. If your opposing team could find an expression equal to 20, it would be worth 3 points: 1 for the 20, 1 for touching the 13, and 1 for touching the 21. You would still get your 2 points, but the opposing team would get 1 point because those players found an expression that resulted in a total number of points worth 1 more point than yours.

11	12	13
19	20	21
27	28	29

› If you are unable to get a number that is unmarked, you score 0 points for the turn. If your opposing team can, that team receives the number of points that its number is worth.
› Play a total of six rounds. The team with the greater total score is the winner.

Unit Fractions and Wholes Rod Models

If Cuisenaire Rods are not available, reproduce this page, cut apart the pieces, and create sets for students to work with.

For opaque bag:

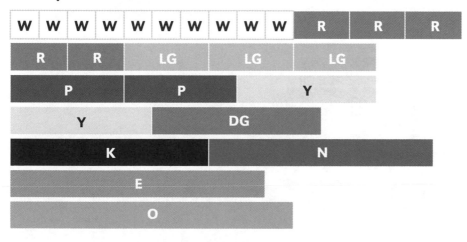

For open collection:

Unit Fractions and Wholes Rod Colors and Letters

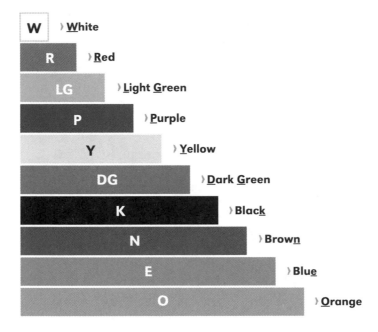

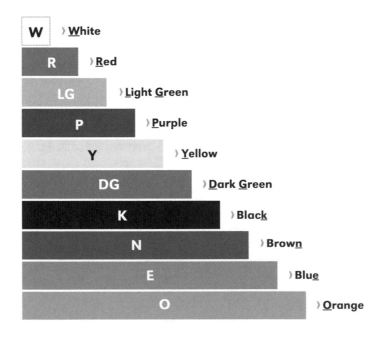

Unit Fractions and Wholes Directions

Materials Needed

› 1 opaque bag containing the following Cuisenaire Rods or 1 set of pieces from the top part of *Unit Fractions and Wholes* Rod Models (page A-65) per group of players: 9 white (W), 5 red (R), 3 light green (LG), 2 purple (P), 2 yellow (Y), 3 dark green (DG), 1 black (K), 3 brown (N), 3 blue (E), and 3 orange (O)

› 1 open collection of Cuisenaire Rods or 1 set of pieces from the bottom part of *Unit Fractions and Wholes* Rod Models per group for students to use to check their thinking (page A-65)

› 1 die per group

› Optional: 1 set of *Unit Fractions and Wholes* Rod Colors and Letters per group (page A-66)

› Optional: 1 *Unit Fractions and Wholes* Directions per group

Directions

Goal: To collect the greater number of pairs of rods.

› Shake the bag of rods to mix them up. Place the bag and open collection of rods in the center of the play area.

› Without looking, each team draws six rods from the bag, one at a time, taking turns. Put the chosen rods in your laps, out of view of the opposing team.

› A member of each team rolls a die and the greater number indicates the team that plays first.

› On each turn, the team chooses one of its rods and decides to identify it as one whole or a unit fraction. Then it asks the opposing team if it has either a certain unit fraction or a whole. For example, if Team 1 chooses a purple rod, and decides that rod will represent one whole, one of the players might say, "This purple rod is one whole. Do you have one-half?"

> › If Team 2 has a red rod, one of its players can say, "Yes, here is the red, which is one-half of the purple." Teams can use the open collection of rods to show this relationship. Team 1 has made a pair and puts the purple and red rods in its pile. Then each team chooses one replacement rod from the bag without looking.

> › If Team 2 does not have a red rod, a member can reply, "No, we don't have a red, which would be one-half of the purple." Team 1 must draw another rod from the bag, and its turn has ended.

> › Note that Team 1 could have chosen the purple rod and said, "This purple rod is one-half. Do you have one whole?" In this case, the other team would check to see if it had a brown rod and show that, since it takes two purples to make a brown, brown would be one whole.

› The game ends when one of the teams no longer has any rods, or there are no more rods in the bag and no matches to be made with the rods the players have left. The winner is the team with the greatest number of pairs.

Name That Number Clues A

The number is a unit fraction.	The denominator of the number is even and less than 10.
The number is not equivalent to $\frac{3}{6}$.	The number is not equivalent to $\frac{2}{8}$.
The number is not $\frac{1}{8}$.	What is the number?

Name That Number Clues B

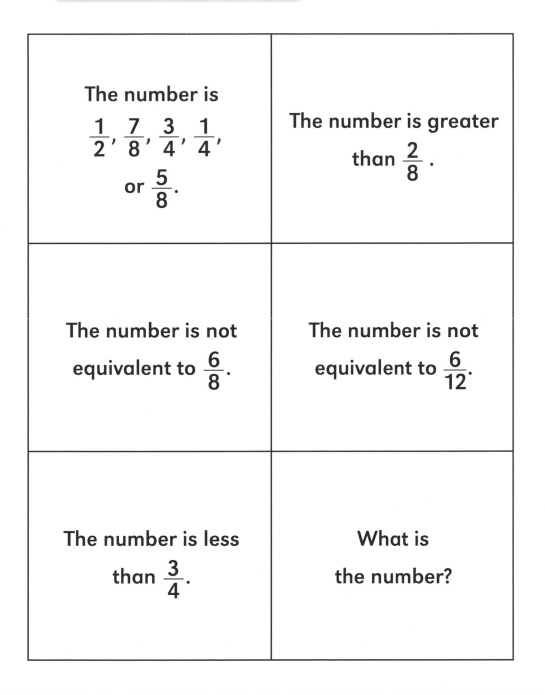

The number is $\frac{1}{2}$, $\frac{7}{8}$, $\frac{3}{4}$, $\frac{1}{4}$, or $\frac{5}{8}$.	The number is greater than $\frac{2}{8}$.
The number is not equivalent to $\frac{6}{8}$.	The number is not equivalent to $\frac{6}{12}$.
The number is less than $\frac{3}{4}$.	What is the number?

Name That Number Clues C

The number is less than 2.	The denominator of the number is even and less than 8.
The numerator of the number is greater than its denominator.	The number is greater than $1\frac{1}{2}$.
The number is less than $7 \times \frac{3}{12}$.	What is the number?

Name That Number Directions

Materials Needed

> 1 set of *Name That Number* Clues A, B, or C per team of three students (page A-68, A-69, or A-70)
> Optional: 1 *Name That Number* Directions per team

Directions

Goal: Use the clues to find the mystery fraction.

> Form a team of three puzzle solvers.

> Place the clues facedown. Each solver randomly takes two of the clues.

> Solvers may read their clues to the others, but may not show the clues.

> Work together to figure out the number being described by the clues. Read the clues as many times as necessary, and talk about what you know.

> You can write or draw to help you understand the information in the clues, but you can't record the clues.

> When you think you have the solution, read the clues again to check.

Order Up Cards

Make two copies of these cards to form one deck.

$\dfrac{0}{2}$	$\dfrac{1}{2}$	$\dfrac{2}{2}$
$\dfrac{0}{3}$	$\dfrac{1}{3}$	$\dfrac{2}{3}$
$\dfrac{3}{3}$	$\dfrac{0}{4}$	$\dfrac{1}{4}$
$\dfrac{2}{4}$	$\dfrac{3}{4}$	$\dfrac{4}{4}$

Order Up Cards (continued)

$\dfrac{0}{6}$	$\dfrac{1}{6}$	$\dfrac{2}{6}$
$\dfrac{3}{6}$	$\dfrac{4}{6}$	$\dfrac{5}{6}$
$\dfrac{6}{6}$	$\dfrac{0}{12}$	$\dfrac{1}{12}$
$\dfrac{2}{12}$	$\dfrac{3}{12}$	$\dfrac{4}{12}$

Order Up Cards (continued)

$\dfrac{5}{12}$	$\dfrac{6}{12}$	$\dfrac{7}{12}$
$\dfrac{8}{12}$	$\dfrac{9}{12}$	$\dfrac{10}{12}$
$\dfrac{11}{12}$	$\dfrac{12}{12}$	$\dfrac{1}{1}$

Order Up Directions

Materials Needed

› 1 deck of *Order Up* Cards per group of players (made from *two* copies of pages A-72–A-74)

› Optional: 1 *Order Up* Directions per group

Directions

Goal: Exchange cards until the five numbers shown in your hand are in order from least to greatest, left to right.

› Shuffle the cards and place five cards faceup, from left to right, in front of each team. Teams may not change the order of the cards in their "hands." Put the remaining cards facedown in the middle of the play area in a seven-by-eight array, as you would in a concentration game.

› Decide who goes first. In this game, there is also an advantage to playing second because you will have seen one of the cards placed facedown in the array.

› You cannot rearrange your cards, but you will be able to exchange your cards for others that may work better in your hand. Note that two cards with equivalent values are not allowed. For example, if you have cards for ¾ and ⅝, you cannot keep both of them, as they have the same value.

› The first team chooses any card from the array and may exchange this card with one of its five cards. If the team chooses to keep the card it has drawn, it puts the card it has removed from its hand facedown in the array to re-place the taken card. If no exchange is made, the team puts the drawn card back in its location in the array.

› Teams take turns picking a card from the board and deciding whether or not to exchange it with a card in their hands.

› The first team to get its five fractions in order from least to greatest is the winner.

Fraction Action Game Board

Name(s): _____ Date: _____

Decide whether teams will try to get the least or greatest sums and differences. You'll receive 1 point each time your sum or difference is the least (or greatest).

Points

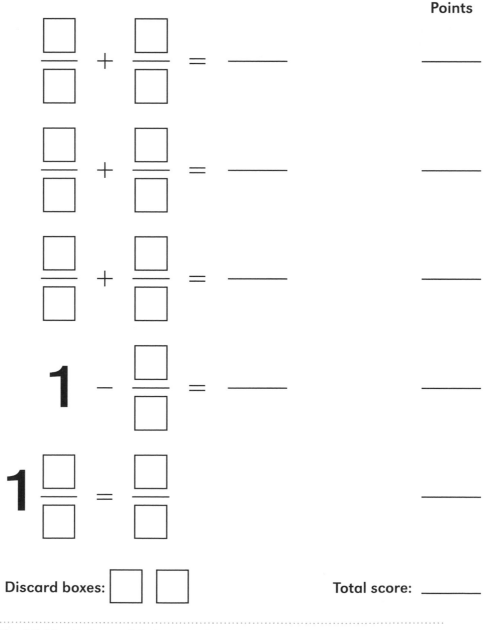

Discard boxes: ☐ ☐   Total score: _____

Fraction Action Cards

Make two copies of the cards to form one deck.

1	1	2	2
3	3	3	4
4	4	5	5
6	6	8	8
10	10	12	12

Fraction Action Directions

Materials Needed

> 1 deck of *Fraction Action* Cards per group of players (made from *two* copies of page A-76)
> 1 *Fraction Action* Game Board per team (page A-77)
> Optional: 1 *Fraction Action* Directions per group

Directions

Goal: Place numerators and denominators in the spaces on the game board, making fractions that—when added or subtracted—form the least or greatest sums and differences.

> Play with two or more teams.
> Shuffle the cards and place them facedown in a pile.
> Decide if the greatest or least sums or differences will receive a point.
> Turn over the top card.
> Each team separately decides in which of the twenty squares on its board to write the number. Be sure to note that two discard squares are available as choices. Once you've written a number, you cannot change it. When everyone has placed the number, turn over the next card.
> Play continues until all twenty squares on the game board have been filled.
> Each team adds and subtracts to complete the equations.
> Compare each sum or difference. The team with the greatest (or least) sum or difference gets 1 point.
> Write your total score. The team with the greatest (or least) total wins.

Well Played: Building Mathematical Thinking Through Number Games and Puzzles, Grades 3–5
by Linda Dacey, Karen Gartland, and Jayne Bamford Lynch. Copyright © 2015. Stenhouse Publishers.

Fraction Jigsaw Puzzle Pieces A

$\frac{5}{10}$ $\frac{7}{8}$	$\frac{1}{2}$ $\frac{2}{8}$ $\frac{1}{6}$	$\frac{1}{4}$ $\frac{2}{6}$	$\frac{1}{3}$ five-eighths
seven-eighths $\frac{2}{4}$ $\frac{1}{2}$	$\frac{1}{2}$ $\frac{3}{6}$ two-thirds	$\frac{3}{8}$ $\frac{1}{2}$ $\frac{4}{4}$ $\frac{1}{8}$	$\frac{5}{8}$ 1
$\frac{2}{3}$ $\frac{1}{4}$	$\frac{2}{3}$ $\frac{4}{6}$ $\frac{3}{1}$ $\frac{5}{6}$	one-eighth 3 $\frac{6}{8}$	$\frac{2}{3}$ $\frac{3}{4}$ $\frac{3}{4}$
$\frac{4}{8}$	$\frac{1}{2}$ $\frac{3}{3}$	$\frac{3}{8}$ 1 $\frac{6}{1}$	three-fourths 6

Fraction Jigsaw Puzzle Pieces B

$3/4$ $3/8 + 1\tfrac{1}{8}$	$9/12$ $\qquad$ $3\tfrac{1}{2}$ (number line: 0 to 1, arrow)	$7/2$ $\qquad$ $2/3$ $1\tfrac{1}{6}$	$8/12$ $3/12 + 9/12$
$1\tfrac{1}{2}$ $7/4$ $2\tfrac{1}{4} + 3/4$	$2/3$ $1\tfrac{3}{4}$ $\qquad$ $4/12$ 2	(number line: 0 to 1, arrow) $1/3$ $\qquad$ $1/2$ $5/8$	1 $5/10$ (number line: 0 to 1, arrow)
3 $4/12$ $1\tfrac{6}{8} - 1/2$	$1\tfrac{4}{8} + 1/2$ $1/3$ $\qquad$ $10/8$ $1\tfrac{1}{2} - 1/8$	$1 - 3/8$ $1\tfrac{1}{4}$ $\qquad$ $6/12$ $2/3$	$1\tfrac{1}{3}$ $1/2$ $1\tfrac{1}{12}$
$1\tfrac{1}{4}$ $4 \times 1/2$ $\qquad$ 2 $\qquad$ $10/12$	$1\tfrac{3}{8}$	(number line: 0 to 1, arrow) $5/6$ $\qquad$ $5 \times 3/5$	$13 \times 1/12$ 3

Fraction Jigsaw Directions

Materials Needed

› 1 set of *Fraction Jigsaw* Puzzle Pieces A or B per group of three to four students (page A-79 or A-80)
› Optional: 1 *Fraction Jigsaw* Directions per group

Directions

Goal: Arrange the puzzle pieces so that the numbers represented on all adjoining sides match.

› Work together.
› Organize all of the sixteen puzzle pieces into a square.
› The pieces should be placed so that the numbers on each of their sides match, that is, so that the numbers on the sides of any adjacent squares have the same value.
› Check to make sure you have matched each side correctly.

Make Your Own *Fraction Jigsaw* Puzzle Pieces Template

Write matching fractions on each side of a square that touches another side of a square. Cut out the pieces and trade with another team.

❯ Puzzle Answer Key

Chapter 4

What's Your Problem?
Extension puzzle answer: A is 4, B is 6, C is 3.

Logical Numbers
Puzzle A—Mica: 545; Cooper: 135; Isabella: 337; Riley: 632; Jordana: 142
Puzzle B—Computer: 11440; front door: 4269; back door: 7987; safe: 2902;
car: 4149; combination lock: 15302

Chapter 5

Matchups
Puzzle A: 11-1, 80-10, 45-9, 32-8, 15-3, 21-7, 50-25, 4-2, 10-5
Puzzle B: 21-3, 310-31, 144-48, 6-2, 100-4, 13-1, 25-5, 700-70, 54-6, 49-7,
150-15, 72-12, 70-10, 33-11, 34-17, 64-8

Chapter 6

Write It Right
(The order of addends or factors may be reversed.)
Puzzle A: $3 + 8 = 11$; $2 + 3 = 5$; $7 \times 9 = 63$; $4 \times 0 = 0$
Puzzle B: $42 \div 6 = 7$; $3 \times 8 = 24$; $0 + 9 = 9$; $5 - 4 = 1$
Puzzle C: $0.2 + 0.3 = 0.5$; $0.1 \times 0.6 \times 100 = 6$; $10 \times 0.4 = 4$ and
$0.2 + 0.3 = 0.5$; $0.1 \times 0.4 \times 100 = 4$; $10 \times 0.6 = 6$

Chapter 7

Name That Number
A: $\frac{1}{6}$; B: $\frac{5}{8}$; C: $\frac{10}{6}$

Back, Jenni. 2013. "Division in Classrooms." *Mathematics Teaching* (September): 10–13.

Blair, Andrew. 2014. "Inquiry Maths: An Idea Whose Time Has Come." *Mathematics Teaching* (May): 32–35.

Bray, Wendy S. 2013. "How to Leverage the Potential of Mathematical Errors." *Teaching Children Mathematics* 19 (7): 424–431.

Broadbent, Frank W. 1972. "Contig: A Game to Practice and Sharpen Skills and Facts on the Four Fundamental Operations." *Arithmetic Teacher* 19 (5): 388–390.

Brock, Sofia, and Alan Edmunds. 2011. "Parental Involvement: Barriers and Opportunities." *The Journal of Educational Administration and Foundations* 20 (1): 1–23.

Burns, Marilyn. 1992. *About Teaching Mathematics.* Sausalito, CA: Math Solutions.

Carpenter, Thomas P., Megan Loef Franke, and Linda Levi. 2003. *Integrating Arithmetic and Algebra in Elementary School.* Portsmouth, NH: Heinemann.

Chapin, Suzanne H., Catherine O'Connor, and Nancy C. Anderson. 2009. *Classroom Discussions: Using Math Talk to Help Students Learn.* 2nd ed. Sausalito, CA: Math Solutions.

Clarke, Doug M., Anne Roche, and Annie Mitchell. 2008. "10 Practical Tips to Make Fractions Come Alive and Make Sense." *Mathematics Teaching in the Middle School* 13 (7): 373–380.

Cooper, Linda L., and Ming C. Tomayko. 2011. "Understanding Place Value." *Teaching Children Mathematics* 17 (9): 558–567.

Cramer, Kathleen A., Thomas R. Post, and Robert C. delMas. 2002. "Initial Fraction Learning by Fourth and Fifth Grade Students: A Comparison of the Effects of Using Commercial Curricula with the Effect of Using the Rational Number Curriculum." *Journal for Research in Mathematics Education* 33 (2): 111–144.

Dacey, Linda, and Anne Collins. 2010. *Zeroing in on Number and Operations: Key Ideas and Common Misconceptions, Grades 3–4.* Portland, ME: Stenhouse.

Dacey, Linda, Jayne Bamford Lynch, and Rebeca Eston Salemi. 2013. *How to Differentiate Your Math Instruction: Lessons, Ideas, and Videos with Common Core Support, Grades K–5.* Sausalito, CA: Math Solutions.

Erickson, Tim. 1989. *Get Together: Math Problems for Groups, 4–12.* Berkeley, CA: Lawrence Hall of Science.

Farbermann, Boris L., and Ruzania G. Musina. 2004. "Picturing the Concepts: An Interactive Teaching Strategy." *Thinking Classroom* 5 (4): 12–16.

Faulkner, Valerie N. 2009. "The Components of Number Sense: An Instructional Model for Teachers." *Teaching Exceptional Children* (41) 5: 24–30.

Fisher, Robert. 2005. *Teaching Children to Think.* 2nd ed. Cheltenham, UK: Nelson Thomes.

Fuson, Karen. 2003. "Toward Computational Fluency in Multidigit Multiplication and Division." *Teaching Children Mathematics* 9 (6): 300–305.

Golembo, Vadim. 2000. "Writing a PEMDAS Story." *Mathematics Teaching in the Middle School* 5 (9): 574–579.

Griffin, Sharon. 2004. "Teaching Number Sense." *Educational Leadership* 61 (5): 39–42.

Hillen, Amy F., and Tad Watanabe. 2013. "Mysterious Subtraction." *Teaching Children Mathematics* 20 (5): 294–301.

Huinker, DeAnn, Janice Freckman, and Meghan Steinmeyer. 2003. "Subtraction Strategies from Children's Thinking: Moving Toward Fluency with Greater Numbers." *Teaching Children Mathematics* 9 (6): 347–353.

Kazemi, Elham, and Allison Hintz. 2014. *Intentional Talk: How to Structure and Lead Productive Mathematical Discussions.* Portland, ME: Stenhouse.

Kliman, Marlene. 2006. "Math Out of School: Families' Math Game Playing at Home." *School Community Journal* 16 (2): 69–90.

Kohlfeld, Carol. 2009. "Playing Games." *Mathematics Teaching* 215 (September): 14–15.

Koster, Ralph. 2013. *A Theory of Fun for Game Design.* 2nd ed. Sebastopol, CA: O'Reilly Media.

Lamon, Susan. 2012. *Teaching Fractions and Ratios for Understanding: Essential Knowledge and Content Strategies for Teachers.* New York: Routledge.

Lan, Yu-Ju, Yao-Ting Sug, Ning-chum Tan, Chiu-Pin Lin, and Kuo-En Chang. 2010. "Mobile-Device-Supported Problem-Based Computational Estimation Instruction for Elementary School Students." *Educational Technology and Society* 13 (3): 55–69.

Lins, Romulo, and James Kaput. 2004. "The Early Development of Algebraic Reasoning: The Current State of the Field." In *The Future of the Teaching and Learning of Algebra: The 12th ICMI Study*, ed. Kaye Stacey, Helen Chick, and Margaret Kendal, 45–70. New ICMI Study Series, vol. 8. Dordrecht, Netherlands: Springer Netherlands.

Mauro, Daniel G., Jo-Anne LeFevre, and Jason Morris. 2003. "Effects of Problem Format on Division and Manipulation Performance: Division Facts Are Mediated via Multiplication-Based Representations." *Journal of Experimental Psychology: Learning, Memory and Cognition* 29 (2): 163–170.

McNeil, Nicole, and Linda Jarvin. 2007. "When Theories Don't Add Up: Disentangling the Manipulatives Debate." *Theory into Practice* 46 (4): 309–316.

Mundia, Lawrence. 2012. "The Assessment of Math Learning Difficulties in a Primary Grade-4 Child with High Support Needs: Mixed Methods Approach." *International Electronic Journal of Elementary Education* 4 (2): 347–366.

National Council of Teachers of Mathematics (NCTM). 2000. *Principles and Standards for School Mathematics.* Reston, VA: NCTM.

National Governors Association Center for Best Practices (NGA) and Council of Chief State School Officers (CCSSO). 2010a. *Common Core State Standards for Mathematics*. Washington, DC: NGA and CCSSO.

——. 2010b. *Reaching Higher: The Common Core State Standards Validation Committee—A Report from the National Governors Association Center for Best Practices and the Council of Chief State School Officers*. Washington, DC: NGA and CCSSO.

National Mathematics Advisory Panel. 2008. *Foundations for Success: The Final Report of the National Mathematics Advisory Panel*. Washington, DC: US Department of Education.

Newman, Rich. 2012. "Goal Setting to Achieve Results." *Leadership* 41 (3): 12–15, 16–18, 38.

Partnership for 21st Century Skills. 2008. *21st Century Skills, Education and Competitiveness: A Resource and Policy Guide*. Tucson, AZ: Partnership for 21st Century Skills.

Psycharis, Giorgos, Maria Latsi, and Chronis Kynigos. 2009. "Meanings for Fraction as Number-Measure by Exploring the Number Line." *The International Journal for Technology in Mathematics Education* 16 (3): 91–107.

Roche, Anne. 2005. "Longer Is Larger—or Is It?" *Australian Primary Mathematics Classroom* 10 (3): 11–16.

Ross, Sharon R. 2002. "Place Value: Problem Solving and Written Assessment." *Teaching Children Mathematics* 8 (7): 419–423.

Schiro, Michael S. 2009. *Mega-fun Games and Puzzles for the Elementary Grades: Over 125 Activities That Teach Math Facts and Concepts*. San Francisco: Jossey-Bass.

Seeley, Cathy. 2004. "A Journey in Algebraic Thinking." *NCTM News Bulletin* (September). Retrieved from http://www.nctm.org/about/content.aspx?id=936.

Siebert, Daniel, and Nicole Gaskin. 2006. "Creating, Naming and Justifying Fractions." *Teaching Children Mathematics* 11 (8): 394–400.

Thouless, Helen. 2014. "Whole-Number Place-Value Understanding of Students with Learning Disabilities." PhD diss., University of Washington.

Torrance, E. Paul. 1974. *The Torrance Tests of Creative Thinking: Norms—Technical Manual*. Bensenville: IL: Scholastic Testing Services.

Van de Walle, John A., Karen Karp, and Jennifer M. Bay-Williams. 2013. *Elementary and Middle School Mathematics: Teaching Developmentally*. 8th ed. New York: Pearson Education.

Varol, Filiz, and Dale C. Farran. 2006. "Early Mathematical Growth: How to Support Your Children's Mathematical Development." *Early Childhood Journal* 33 (6): 381–387.

Wedekind, Kassia Omohundro. 2011. *Math Exchanges: Guiding Young Mathematicians in Small-Group Meetings*. Portland, ME: Stenhouse.

Yang, Der Jing, Robert Reys, and Li Lin Wu. 2010. "Comparing the Development of Fractions in the Fifth and Sixth Graders' Textbooks of Singapore, Taiwan, and the USA." *School Science and Mathematics* 110 (3): 118–127.